Date Due

D1174408

6

THOMAS BREDIN

From Sea to Sea:

Alexander Mackenzie

Longman Canada Limited

To the memory of
WALTER BURMAN, 1880-1947
Headmaster, 1913-1946,
St. John's College School, Winnipeg.

Copyright © 1970 Thomas Bredin

Longman Canada Limited
55 Barber Greene Road
Don Mills, Ontario

Set in 10 on 13 pt. Times Roman
Paper: 60 lb. Trade Book Antique
Printed in Canada by The Hunter Rose Company

Contents

Author's note

ALEXANDER MACKENZIE told his own story. He began writing it at Fort Chepewyan after his return from the Pacific. "I find it a work that will require more time than I was aware of." The *Voyages* was published in 1801. The book contains neither "embellished narrative" nor "animated description," neither "exaggeration" nor "display." He was not, he wrote, " a candidate for literary fame"; he claimed only the approval "due to simplicity and to truth."

Others have told Mackenzie's story, of course, since it is worth telling. Some of these accounts say that Mackenzie's journal was ghost-written by William Combe. The evidence for this statement seems to be based on a list of "ghost-written" manuscripts which Combe gave to an admirer. Included in the list is *Sir Alexander Mackenzie's Voyage to South America*! The British Museum cannot trace such a volume—obviously.

Even if Mackenzie did get the assistance of a professional writer, the manner of writing and much of the content has a limited appeal and interest today.

So, in this book about Mackenzie's journeys, I have edited the original. I have cut out quite a bit. I have occasionally changed words or phrasing—always reluctantly. Sentences have been shortened and punctuation revised. However I have not indicated the trimming by the customary three dots and I have kept quotation marks while changing style. After all, it is still Mackenzie's work.

My sole intent was to let Mackenzie tell his own story again —more briefly, and in a fashion less unfamiliar to present-day readers.

Certain books, institutions and persons have been indispensable in shaping this account of Mackenzie's travels, and I would like to acknowledge them. Chief among the books are

M. S. Wade's biography of Mackenzie, L. R. Masson's and G. C. Davidson's books on the North West Company, H. A. Innis's works on Peter Pond and the fur trade, and some volumes from the wonderful publications of the Champlain Society and Hudson's Bay Record Society. Those superlative repositories of information and skilled staff, the Public Archives of Canada and the British Museum, supplied answers to many queries. Miss Marjorie Morley was generous with her time and the resources of the Manitoba Legislative Library. And, of course, I owe a general thanks to the students of St. John's-Ravenscourt School.

Thomas Bredin

Chapter one

Fortunes in fur

I~N~ 1779 A HOMELESS, wandering young Scot arrived in Montreal, a French-Canadian outpost of several thousands on the edge of the wilderness. Its few English-speaking merchants, so often of Scottish descent, made their money in the fur trade. Like his countrymen, Alexander Mackenzie had come to find his fortune too. He was sixteen.

When he was twelve, he and his father, a widower, had left Stornoway in the Outer Hebrides for America. The quarrels between Britain and the thirteen colonies were then approaching their armed climax. During the American Revolution, he set out from New York for the untroubled St. Lawrence. There are no detailed records of Mackenzie's early life, and all he himself says is that he found employment in "the counting-house of Mr. Gregory."

Here let us leave the youth, settled for a while in humble apprenticeship: fetching and carrying, unbaling and packing trade goods or furs, putting things on warehouse shelves or removing them, sorting and counting stock, running errands, and even perhaps being introduced to the mysteries of bookkeeping. As he was busy earning and learning, events elsewhere were shaping opportunities for his driving energy and growing ambition.

Twenty years before young Mackenzie began his modest labours, three thundering volleys from eighteen hundred British muskets on the Plains of Abraham had sounded the fall of New France. In the year of his birth, 1763, the Treaty of Paris transferred possession of the St. Lawrence to the British Crown.

The colony's chief export was fur, freighted by canoe from posts as distant as those built by the La Vérendrye family, father and sons, on Manitoba rivers: the Winnipeg, the Assiniboine and the Saskatchewan. In fact, as the British invasion fleet neared Quebec in June 1759, François de La Vérendrye came down the Ottawa with western pelts and twelve hundred Indian allies. The trading forts on the perimeter of the prairies, referred to as La Mer de l'Ouest posts, were abandoned during the Seven Years' War and the flow of fur out of the St. Lawrence was checked.

The stoppage was only temporary. Accompanying the invading and occupying British armies, to supply them with food and drink, to stock, to service and to run canteens and taverns, were several hundred Scottish and American traders. Some of them were not long in discovering the profit possibilities of the Indian, or fur, trade. Unemployed for the moment, but readily available, were hardy French canoemen, skilled interpreters, guides, clerks, and the knowledgeable bourgeois or "bosses." The portage paths alongside the river routes west were silent and untrodden.

Not for long. The London market for fur was open. Prices were attractive. The Indians, dependent now on guns, powder and shot for survival, needed trade goods. Money invested by Quebec's and Montreal's new English-speaking inhabitants— Gregory's firm was one of many—revived the trade based since Champlain's time on the St. Lawrence.

At first the British equipped and financed expeditions managed by former French traders. In 1767, for example, of eleven canoes licensed to trade from or beyond Kaministiquia, "the river of difficult entrance" at the west end of Lake Superior, nine were commanded by French bourgeois, some of whom had wintered years before in the Northwest. One, the veteran François le Blanc, may have travelled with the La Vérendryes.

Fortunes were made. There was Thomas Corry, who with French guides and interpreters "acquainted with the country" got as far as La Vérendrye's Fort Bourbon on Cedar Lake in northern Manitoba. Corry made several expeditions and eventually "came back with his canoes filled with fine furs and was satisfied never again to return to the Indian country." He made enough money to live comfortably for the rest of his life.

Then there was James Finlay. He wintered not far from the forks of the Saskatchewan River in 1768-69, "where he is said to have cleared upwards of Three thousand pounds in one winter." Philip Turnor, who made this observation in 1779, was then employed as a surveyor by the Hudson's Bay Company. At fifty pounds a year he was one of its better-paid servants, which gives some indication of Finlay's gain. Finlay retired, more or less, to become an inspector of chimneys in Montreal.

So, by using "old standing Traders" and Canadian personnel who "have great Command over the Indians"; by employing the tough little voyageurs, "chosen Men inured to hardship & fatigue"; and by intercepting Indian canoes en route with pelts to H.B.C. posts, an increasing number of English-speaking traders, backed almost completely by British money, were gaining control of the Northwest.

As the fortune-hunting newcomers acquired northern experience, as Montreal companies merged, broke up, and reorganized in the profit-seeking struggle, and as more and more young Scottish and English apprentices—but mostly Scots like Mackenzie—found employment in an expanding business, the French were restricted mainly to clerk and voyageur status. The bourgeois of Canadian origin were gradually elbowed aside. A few tried to operate independently, but they were eventually overwhelmed by numbers, greater financial resources, and business manoeuvering.

In 1774 Thomas and Joseph Frobisher carried the St. Lawrence trade to the Churchill River and beyond its former French boundaries. The two brothers thereby set in motion a series of events that was to extend Quebec and Montreal affairs to the shores of the Pacific. They had arrived on the road to a new and rich fur-bearing region—the Athabasca country—where young Mackenzie was to realize his hopes.

The Frobishers followed the Churchill only as far west as Lake

Ile à la Crosse in northern Saskatchewan. For several years they sent wintering parties to the Churchill to halt and barter with the Athabasca Indians on their annual journey to Fort Prince of Wales at the river's mouth. Trade canoes from the St. Lawrence reached the Churchill in the late fall and departed with furs for Montreal early the next summer, passing on the way another Frobisher-financed brigade heading northwest.

The brothers staked out the Churchill River as their personal business domain, and while their employees were there, intruders could be and were warned off. But approximately from the end of May to the beginning of October, which was the non-trading season, their northern establishments were vacant, and the gate was open for rival traders to travel further up the Churchill and intercept the Indians on their way to the Frobishers.

Or even to build a post right in the Athabasca country. It was bound to happen. The haul of fur from the Churchill made up as much as 10% of all the pelts shipped out of the St. Lawrence and was immensely profitable. The trader who slipped onto the Churchill just after the canoes of the Frobishers left in 1778 and who blazed the path to Lake Athabasca was Peter Pond.

Connecticut-born Pond, whose career was briefly to join and greatly to influence Mackenzie's, was a veteran traveller who boasted that the first three years of his marriage "was the ondley three years of my life I was three years in one place sins I was sixteen years old up to sixty." At sixteen, quitting a shoemaker apprenticeship, he became a soldier in the Seven Years' War, caught like many a lad by "the drums an instraments of Musick," rising through the ranks from private to sergeant to officer by 1760. After his stint of fighting, "a Voige to the islands in the West Indies," and a brief trial of married life, he entered the fur trade at Detroit in 1765, where he killed a man in a duel. Later he was circumstantially linked with the slaying of two rival traders in the Northwest.

One of his countrymen, Alexander Henry, referred to Pond as "a trader of some celebrity in the Northwest." Since Henry himself was a renowned adventurer—he had escaped massacre at Michilimackinac and trampling by a buffalo herd in a prairie blizzard—it was a big compliment.

Pond first went into the Northwest—"technically," said Alexander Henry, "the country northwest of Lake Superior"—in 1775 and wintered at Fort Dauphin in Manitoba. The following two winters he spent on the upper Saskatchewan.

The Frobishers had interests there, too, and of course their success on the Churchill was no secret. "In the spring of the year 1778, some of the traders on the Saskatchewine river, finding they had a quantity of goods to spare, agreed to put them into a joint stock, and gave the charge and management of them to Mr. Peter Pond, who was directed to enter the English River [the Churchill], so called by Mr. Frobisher, to follow his track and proceed still further; if possible, to Athabasca, a country hitherto unknown but from Indian report." This brief account, by the way, is from a history of the fur trade written by Alexander Mackenzie.

Another observer reported Pond's progress. He was William Tomison, master of Cumberland House on the Saskatchewan River. This fort was the first built in the interior by the Hudson's Bay Company to meet Montreal competition. Tomison wrote in his journal on May 26, 1778: "At noon Peter Pond one of the Canadian traders arrived here with five large Canoes loaded with Goods; He is going to penetrate into the A,tho,pus,cow country as far as he can possibly go and there to stay this next Winter."

Later, in September, Tomison's journal recorded the arrival just below Cumberland House of two traders named Primeau and St. Germain. "The former wintered last Year in the Beaver Lake, the latter is come from Montreal this Summer; they intend to proceed nigh hand to the A,tho,pus,cow Country where Primo wintered two Years ago. They are in the employ of Mr. Frobisher and Partners."

Pond had stolen a three-month march on them.

The scene changes. While Pond was paddling into the untapped fur-bearing regions of the Athabasca, Captain James Cook, famed explorer of the South Pacific, was mapping the northwest coast of the American continent. The discoveries of the two men were to become intertwined and to involve the young Mackenzie, who had not yet turned his steps towards Mr. Gregory's counting-house in Montreal.

The main purpose of Cook's voyage was to examine closely the northern shores of America and to search for an east-west link between the Pacific and the Atlantic. To any British subject who succeeded in finding a sailing passage north of latitude 52° joining the two oceans, Parliament offered a reward of £20,000.

On March 30, 1778, Cook's two ships, the *Resolution* and the *Discovery*, anchored in Nootka Sound, roughly midway on the west coast of Vancouver Island, where he remained nearly a month. On that and on succeeding days, fleets of native canoes brought the skins of "bears, wolves, foxes, deer, racoons, pole-cats, martens; and in particular, the sea otters" and took in exchange "knives, chisels, pieces of iron and tin, nails, looking-glasses, buttons, or any kind of metal. Copper kettles, tin canisters, candlesticks, and the like, all went to wreck."

The two ships left Nootka, coasted towards the north, and at the end of May entered a long channel or inlet which was explored northeastward until it narrowed to four leagues and then to one. "As we proceeded farther up the marks of a river displayed themselves. The water was found to be fresher. I was convinced that we were in a larger river, and not in a strait connecting with the Northern Seas." He called it River Turn-again.

Cook then rounded the Alaskan Peninsula, and penetrated Bering Strait almost to Point Barrow before finding the ships' way blocked by ice. On their return to winter in the Sandwich—now the Hawaiian—Islands which they had discovered earlier in the year, they visited Russian traders at Oonalashka Island in the Bering Sea near the Alaskan coast. "Their great object is the sea beaver or otter."

In February 1779 Cook was murdered by some natives on

one of the Hawaiian Islands. Those who succeeded to his command visited Russian trade establishments around Kamtschatka on the northern Asiatic coast, and again attempted to enter the Canadian Arctic. Getting only about as far as Cook had the previous year, the *Resolution* and *Discovery* were pointed south for the return journey to England. They stopped at Canton, in China, which was thought to be "the most advantageous market for the furs" that they had gathered in the Northern Pacific.

Here "one of our seamen sold his stock for eight hundred dollars; and a few prime skins, which were clean and well-preserved, were sold for one hundred and twenty each. The rage with which our seamen were possessed to return, and by another cargo of skins to make their fortunes at one time, was not far short of mutiny." Pelts which had sold for so much in Canton had cost no more than sixpence at Nootka. But the sailors were denied the opportunity of quickly filling their pockets with cash; the ships set home and arrived in England by the fall of 1780.

River Turnagain came to be known as Cook's River; and it had been the captain's opinion that "by means of this river, and its several branches, a very extensive inland communication seems to be open." If the eastern headwaters of "this great river" could be found, they might provide an exit from the American land mass to the rich seal and otter grounds. Peter Pond came to believe that he knew the way.

How had that Yankee trader fared?

Just more than a year later, Pond returned and rested overnight at Cumberland House. Tomison wrote: "At noon arrived Mr. Petter Pond with three Canoes from the Northward. He was so far that he traded with the Northward Indians that Mr. Samuel Hearne was along with, Mit'tee'na'pew and his gang, He has been two Summers upon this voiage made 140 Packs each 90 lbs. but was obliged to leave the most part of them behind, mostly parchment and Coat beaver He informed me of one carrying Place to be about 12 miles over being so steep They was eight days a Carrying over it. He had even traded his Cloath's off his Back."

The carrying place was the Methye Portage, north of Ile à la

Crosse, and between Methye Lake and the Clearwater River. It traversed the height of land separating Arctic and Hudson Bay waters. Philip Turnor crossed it in May 1792 and described the path in some detail. He estimated the whole portage at about fifteen miles, mostly through gently rising pine woods, but sometimes over swampy ground or grassy meadows. According to him the most precarious section of the hike was several hundred yards of up and down trail on a ridge "about two yards wide at the top the sides of which are very steep and not less than a Hundred yards to the bottom on either side and if a person was to make a slip to either side he would be shure of being at the bottom before he stoped."

Pond's observations have not survived on paper. He had travelled along the Clearwater to the Athabasca River, and on its east bank, about thirty or forty miles south of Lake Athabasca, built a fort. For ten years it served as his trading headquarters.

On a visit to Montreal in 1785, Pond learned from the published narratives about Cook's Pacific coast explorations—about Cook's Inlet, Cook's River, and the China trade possibilities. He himself had by then learned something of the geography of the country north of his fort: of Lake Athabasca, of its Slave River drainage to Slave Lake. He added Cook's discoveries to his own crude map of the Northwest, and returned to his distant winter quarters, fired by the prospects of finding a connection with Cook's River, harvesting the sea beaver, and marketing the skins across the Pacific in China.

Ships had already left American ports by 1784 and sailed round Cape Horn for the northern Pacific coast. An American enterprise of 1786-87 obtained 2,552 skins which sold in China for $54,857.

A race for wealth and empire was on, and just at that moment Alexander Mackenzie's apprenticeship in Gregory's counting-house was completed. He became a trader himself.

Chapter two

Bourgeois and voyageur

By 1784 MACKENZIE had so impressed his employer that he was sent "with a small adventure of goods to seek my fortune at Detroit" as an active trader. Later in the year he was offered a partnership in the business "on condition that I would proceed to the Indian country in the following spring, 1785." Indian country was the Northwest. Mackenzie accepted, met his colleagues at Grand Portage at the western end of Lake Superior, and from here set out with his cousin Roderick McKenzie to trade on the Churchill River.

Meanwhile in 1783-84 "the traders in the country and the merchants at Montreal entered into a co-partnership." They called themselves the North West Company; "the management of the whole was entrusted to Messrs. Benjamin and Joseph Frobisher and Mr. Simon M'Tavish." McTavish, who came to America as a boy in 1764 with nothing, was by 1800 so much the dominant figure in the N.W.Co., and a very rich man, that he was nicknamed "the Premier" and "the Marquis."

This company's aim was to monopolize the Montreal-Grand Portage-Northwest business. Gregory and his associate Macleod were not included in the five-year arrangement, nor was the trader Peter Pangman. Together they decided to challenge the bigger company, with which Pond, originally left out also, had made a personally acceptable deal.

The smaller company was licensed in 1785 to send eight canoes into the Northwest with trade goods valued at £5,600 and in 1786 another eight carrying £4,500 worth. Pangman, Mackenzie, and a John Ross were among the winterers in charge. "After the severest struggle ever known in that part of the world;

after the murder of one of our partners, the laming of another, and the narrow escape of one of our clerks who received a bullet through his powder horn, the North West Company were compelled to allow us a share of the trade. This union was concluded in July, 1787." The murdered man was John Ross. Linked with his killing was Peter Pond.

The new N.W.Co., enlarged in 1787 so as to include Gregory, Macleod and their winterers, was formed for seven years. Its twenty shares, four of which went to Gregory, Macleod, Pangman and Mackenzie, were held by two kinds of partners: the agents at Montreal who managed the business in Canada, and the proprietors or bourgeois who with their clerks "were obliged to winter and to manage the business with the Indians."

Shares in the company could not be bought by just anybody with the ready cash. "No persons could be admitted as a partner who had not served his time in the trade." "From their long services and influence" some held two shares; most owned but one. A double shareholder could retire as a "dormant partner," keeping one share and "naming any young man in the company's service to succeed him in the other." So the apprentices, who bound themselves to the company for five to seven years as clerks at a hundred pounds a year with food and clothing, could hope to become partners some day too. The practice encouraged ambition; it rewarded ability and hard work. Although there might be complaints that it was mostly friends, relatives and pull that opened the doors to advancement, the choice of a new partner had to be approved by a majority of shareholders.

Of course a share was purchased from a retiring associate at the going price. It was part of the total value of goods and furs on hand. In 1788 single shares were worth £800; by 1799, £2,400; and in 1802, £3,300. There were twenty shares in 1788, but by 1802 there were nearly a hundred. The company prospered.

Every summer, agents and proprietors assembled at Grand Portage. When American customs officials began to interfere with their operations because Grand Portage was found to be in

United States territory, the partners built a new depot at Fort William.

At this annual meeting the post managers told the agents what kinds and amounts of trade goods were needed. When they got back to Montreal the agents ordered these things from England and received them into the company warehouses the next summer. During the fall and winter the goods were made up into ninety-pound packages and after the spring break-up they were shipped by canoe brigade to Grand Portage. Two of the agents always made the summer journey with them while at the same time the wintering partners urged fleets of fur eastward.

A great variety of trade goods was imported by the agents for the company's Indian customers: "coarse woolen cloths of different kinds; milled blankets of different sizes; arms and ammunition; twists and carrot tobacco; Manchester goods; linens, and coarse sheetings; thread, lines, and twine; common hardware; cutlery and ironmongery of several descriptions; kettles of brass and copper, and sheet-iron; silk and cotton handkerchiefs, hats, shoes and hose; calicoes and printed cottons. Spirituous liquors and provisions are purchased in Canada." In this long list, the largest single cargo item carried by the canoes was kegs of rum and wine, and the next was powder, shot and guns.

In exchange for these wares, enormous quantities of fur poured out of the Northwest. In 1799, according to Mackenzie, there were 184,300 skins, more than half of which were beaver. One unusual fur exported from Quebec was "tyger" which, whatever it was, after a peak of 172 skins diminished to one skin and then to none. The beaver pelts alone made up more than 1,500 hundred-pound packs, or about seventy-five tons of freight, which was moved from all the interior trading posts to Grand Portage in birch bark canoes.

Plainly, the N.W.Co. was a fair-sized operation. Freighting and trading occupied considerable numbers of men by the mid-1790s. Mackenzie, who doesn't say what year, gives the following figures: "fifty clerks, seventy-one interpreters and clerks, one thousand and twenty canoe-men, and thirty-five guides."

Of the canoemen, 350 were hired in Montreal and employed from the beginning of May to the end of September on the Montreal-Grand Portage-Montreal run. Hence they were called the "Goers and Comers," or "Porkeaters." The remainder, who worked in the Northwest, were called "North Men or Winterers." And attached to this group were "upwards of seven hundred Indian women and children, victualled at the expense of the company."

The paddling and toting proletariat consisted of the foremen, who were in command, were always on the lookout, and directed the canoe; steersmen, who attended the helm—a highly skilled job on swift-running rivers; and the middlemen, who took orders from both. Their assorted summer sufferings included carrying canoes and cargo on their backs along the portage trails.

About forty to fifty canoes, forty-odd feet in length, with a four-ton capacity, were used to transport goods and furs between Montreal and Grand Portage. They were made of birch bark a quarter of an inch thick stretched over a frame of vertical ribs fastened to the gunwales. The different parts were sewn together with *watape*, "the divided roots of the spruce fir." Horizontal slats of white cedar lined the interior, and bars rather than seats ran from gunwale to gunwale. A gummy material, made by boiling the pitch from pine trees, was pressed along the outer seams and joins of the completed craft. When it hardened, the canoe was watertight and ready for use.

Near the beginning of May when the lakes and rivers were usually free of ice, the North West Company canoes set out just above the Lachine Rapids, then eight miles west of Montreal. The cargo was carefully loaded on the "grand perch," a set of four three-inch poles running the length of the canoe and resting on the ribs so that no weight pressed on the bark shell.

In each canoe, by Mackenzie's account, were "eight or ten men and their baggage; and sixty-five packages of goods, six hundred weight of biscuit, two hundred weight of pork, three bushels of pease, for the men's provision; two oil-cloths to cover the goods, a sail, etc., an axe, a towing-line, a kettle, and a sponge to bail out the water, with a quantity of gum, bark, and *watape*, to repair the vessel."

Thus heaped up with more than three tons of cargo and supplies, the canoe sank to within six inches of the water when the crew took their places. These long, slender, gracefully curved craft bore their burden over a sometimes rough and rugged watery road. So perilous was it that one observer wrote that the Montreal traders "seldom come in with the loss of less than one tenth of their Canoes, and often lose goods and all"—meaning by "all," the men.

Between Lachine and Georgian Bay Mackenzie counted upwards of thirty portages, totalling not far short of fifteen thousand paces, where the canoe and all its lading had to be carried around rocks, falls or rapids. At a décharge—a shallow stretch—the canoe was towed with one man in the stern "to keep it in the proper channel," though sometimes if the water was low the canoe had to be lightened and part of the load carried.

John Johnston, a Sault Ste. Marie trader, described the carrying technique at portages:

This is done by means of leather straps or thongs, the middle of which is broad and fitted to the forehead of the carrier. The first bale or piece is tied so as to lie a little above the *reins* (the back). The second is lifted over the head and deposited, without tying, on the first.* Thus loaded, the *engagés*, as they are called, trot off to the place chosen for a deposit, which they call a *pose*, and which, in large portages, are from two to three miles apart. This they repeat till the whole is transported. They then go back for the canoe which they carry on their shoulders. They so go on till night, only stopping once for their meal and once or twice for lighting their pipes. He is not looked upon as "a man" who cannot carry two; there are many who even take three and outrun their fellows.

---

*It rested on the hollow of the neck and balanced the ninety-pound pull on the forehead band.

The portage at Sault Ste. Marie was half a mile and the Grand Portage at the far end of Lake Superior was nine miles. From here to Rainy Lake were more than thirty carrying-places, and the Winnipeg River draining Lake of the Woods was punctuated with the labours of unloading, carrying, reloading, unloading, carrying and reloading. Its navigation, about 160 miles, was interrupted "by 37 Portages of varying lengths," and at one spot, just before Lac du Bonnet, "are seven portages in so short a space that the whole of them are discernible at the same moment." Between Lake Winnipeg and Lake Athabasca the way was so tortured with carrying that Mackenzie, in describing the canoe route from Montreal to Fort Chipewyan, eventually gave up listing the names and distances of portage places.

A portage could be as short as twenty-five paces, like the Portage des Allumettes on the Ottawa River, or even a brief fifteen paces. The longest was the steep, twelve-mile Methye Portage.

Length mattered. Over a short carrying-place the eight or ten voyageurs might carry the whole four-ton load on one trip, four or five hundred pounds per man, then return for the canoe. Over the Portage du Bonnet on the Winnipeg River, "near half a league in length," Mackenzie says that "there have been examples of men taking seven packages of ninety pounds each, at one end of the portage, and putting them down at the other without stopping." Over the longer trails such exhibitionist feats of strength were not humanly possible; two trips were needed to move the whole cargo.

What really mattered was the character of the portage road. On the first Portage de Chaudière, near the present site of Ottawa, "the rock is so steep and difficult of access, that it requires twelve men to take the canoe out of the water. It is then carried by six men, two at each end and two in the middle." It was 643 paces long. On the Portage Mauvais de Musique, which was by the Mattawa River between the Ottawa and Lake Nipissing, "many men have been crushed to death by the canoes, and others have received irrecoverable injuries." The new Grand

Portage, west of *the* Grand Portage, "three thousand one hundred paces in length, and over very rough ground, requires the utmost exertions of the men and frequently lames them."

The great canoes from Montreal generally arrived at the Grand Portage by the beginning of July. Each of the Goers and Comers now had to carry "eight packages of such goods and provisions as are necessary for the interior" across the nine-mile portage. It had sixteen *poses* or intermediate depots. At the western end of the portage was Fort Charlotte. "If more goods have to be transported, they are allowed a Spanish dollar for each package. I have known some of them set off with two packages of ninety pounds each and return with two others of the same weight in six hours."

Some goods and furs were moved to and from Grand Portage on batteaux poled from Montreal to Kingston, by sailing ship from here to Niagara, where they were carried around the falls and then loaded onto ships for Sault Ste. Marie and Lake Superior. In 1797-98 a lock was built by the North West Company to get around the rapids at Sault Ste. Marie and into the upper lake. This lock was destroyed in the War of 1812.

In Mackenzie's time it took a little over two weeks to hump more than one hundred tons of trade-goods packages to Fort Charlotte and as much fur to the edge of Lake Superior. Horses and oxen had been "tried by the company without success"; men could do the work more efficiently.

Under certain circumstances the Montreal canoemen might have a rest after these tiring marches. It depended on the time of break-up in the different parts of the country. Usually the North men appeared with their loads of fur early in July, and were ready to return with trade goods to their respective winter quarters within a fortnight. The canoes and paddlers from Athabasca, "owing to the shortness of the season and length of road," came only as far as Rainy Lake. Some of the Goers and Comers took trade goods to them and brought back their furs.

The most complete description of the Grand Portage fort was given by trader John Macdonell. In his retirement he wrote down, as well as he could remember, what it looked like in 1793. It was situated on gently rising ground "in the bottom of a shallow Bay perhaps three miles deep and about four to five miles wide at its mouth." A wharf or pier ran out into the bay and near it was a canoe yard which turned out seventy vessels a year.

The palisaded enclosure, "not above fifteen to twenty paces from the waters edge," measured four hundred by about six hundred feet, or a space very nearly equal that of four regulation football fields. In this area were sixteen buildings.

Six of these buildings are Store Houses for the company's Merchandize and Furs &c. The rest are dwelling houses shops compting house and Mess House.

The Gates are shut alyways after sunset and the Bourgeois and clerks Lodge in houses within the pallisades, where there are two Sentries keeping a look out all night for fear of accident by fire. The North men while here live in tents of different sizes pitched at random, the people of each post having a camp by themselves and through their camp passes the road of the portage. They are separated from the Montrealeans by a brook.

While here, the rations of the canoemen, who numbered sometimes as many as twelve hundred, consisted solely of Indian corn and melted fat. A quart of corn was boiled for two hours in a gallon of water, two ounces of melted suet was added, and the corn, which split as it cooked, made "a pretty thick pudding." This dish, costing less than ten pence, was "fully sufficient for a man's subsistence during twenty-four hours."

The administrative and executive personnel enjoyed a more varied fare. Up to a hundred clerks, guides and interpreters ate with the properietors in one large hall. On the tables were "bread, salt pork, beef, hams, fish, venison, butter, peas, Indian corn, potatoes, tea, spirits, wine, etc." Cows were kept for milk and a large vegetable garden was cultivated around the palisade.

For the few days that wintering partners and agents were together, they had a lot of business to get through. North men were selected and recruited from among the Porkeaters. Contracts of other North men were renewed on a one-, two-, or three-year basis; their accounts were settled and arrangements made to send their earnings home to wives or relatives in Canada. The proprietors and agents had a profit or loss to declare on a previous year's operations; earnings to distribute; exploration, expansion, market conditions, Hudson's Bay Company competition, and the opening of new posts to discuss; promotions, allocation of personnel, the retirement of old and appointment of new partners to consider.

Much of the information which the agents had to digest, such as the condition and outlook of the interior trade, inventories and requirements of goods at particular posts, employees' indebtedness, provisioning, and so on, was sent to Grand Portage by winter express. Men left the most northerly posts about January and travelled by sled and snowshoe through the whole country. About April they converged on Grand Portage. The proprieors' newsletters and reports which they had picked up on the way were then summarized for the annual meeting.

When they had finished with these affairs, the wintering partners returned with their men to their districts. David Thompson, surveying pupil of Philip Turnor and later an explorer, mapmaker and trader-partner with the N.W.Co., says that the canoes "for the most distant trading posts are sent off first;—with an allowance of two days time between each Brigade to prevent encumbrances on the Carrying Places." It was humiliating to be caught by a pursuing brigade.

The canoes of the North were much smaller than the Montreal-Grand Portage freighters. Paddled by four to six men, they were twenty-four to twenty-seven feet long, about five wide and two deep. Their capacity was two to three tons. On the average each carried thirty-five packages, of which twenty-three, a bit more than a ton and a half, were trade goods. So, a huge fleet of approximately 125 canoes, with a pilot or conductor in charge of every four or six vessels, was on the water between the fur posts and Rainy Lake or Grand Portage each summer.

Returning with the Athabasca brigade in 1787 was Alexander Mackenzie, only twenty-four, a brand-new N.W.Co. partner recently appointed to join Peter Pond in the rich Athabasca trade department.

The journey was almost not completed. Winter set in early and for five days the canoes were held by ice on the Churchill River "30 leagues" before Ile à la Crosse. They proceeded slowly, "being frequently obliged to break the ice." At the end of the Methye Portage the ice was running so thick in the Clearwater "that there was no possibility of pulling a canoe in it." Mackenzie cached the trade goods and sent his men to the portage fort to winter. It was then just the middle of October.

"On the 17th, the weather getting milder, and the ice running not quite so thick, I got eight of my men to embark with me in a light canoe. These men left their own things and with great difficulty and risk we arrived at Athabasca the night of the 25th."

After a voyage of nearly fifteen hundred miles Mackenzie had reached Pond's establishment on the Athabasca River. Here the two men passed together the long, slack, snow-bound months.

Chapter three

"*The compleatest inland house*"

Pond had remained at Athabasca since returning there in the fall of 1785. From clerks trading at Slave Lake to the north, from travels of his own, or from Indian customers, Pond learned more about Slave Lake and found out about a great river that flowed towards the Pacific from its western end. This river he located on his map of the Northwest. He showed it running southwest towards Cook's River and along its north bank was printed the phrase, "A Great Waterfall." A stream called the "River of the Mountains" (the Liard) was shown flowing into it from the south.

Certainly Pond hoped that he would be able to explore out of Slave Lake towards the Pacific. During the winter the older man spent some time revising his Northwest map and Mackenzie became completely familiar with Pond's geographical notions. More than that happened. Pond's theories so excited Mackenzie that, if there was going to be a company-financed Pacific exploring party, he wanted to be its captain.

Suddenly in December or January, Mackenzie left Athabasca and snowshoed three hundred miles from Pond's House to Ile à la Crosse where his cousin, Roderick McKenzie, was clerk. At Ile à la Crosse Mackenzie spoke to the partner there about Pond's "wild ideas of matters." What is meant by "matters" is not certain, but Pond was reported to be "preparing a fine map to lay before the Empress of Russia." To his cousin, Alexander offered a position as clerk at Athabasca, which Roderick, who was undecided about remaining in the Northwest, refused.

In a letter sent to Roderick as he tramped back to Athabasca, Mackenzie wrote: "I have already mentioned to you some of my distant intentions. I beg you will not reveal them to any person as it might be prejudicial to me, though I may never have it in my power to put them into execution." By "intentions" Mackenzie meant for one a voyage to the Pacific, because that is what he later attempted—with Roderick's support.

If Mackenzie intended to make not only Pond's ambitions, but that man's trading district as well, his very own, then several favourable circumstances requiring the approval of the majority of the partners at Grand Portage were necessary. First, Mackenzie would have to be posted back to Athabasca and Pond would have to go elsewhere or lie fallow for a year; one proprietor to a department was the company custom. Second, the partners would have to sanction the journey and supply the expenses of exploration. To realize these intentions, Mackenzie had sufficient support in his pocket by July, after the annual summer meeting of the partners.

The report of a talk in July between Alexander and his cousin at Rainy Lake confirms the success of Mackenzie's intrigues. Years later Roderick settled at Terrebonne in Lower Canada, married a French-Canadian girl, reared a bilingual family, and gathered traders' journals, reminiscences and letters for a history of the fur trade which he never wrote. A granddaughter married L. F. R. Masson and the collection, which came into his hands, he edited and published in 1889 under the title *Les Bourgeois de la Compagnie du Nord-Ouest*.

In this book, Roderick's account of the July rendezvous at Rainy Lake is that Alexander told him "in confidence, that he had determined on undertaking a voyage of discovery the ensuing spring by the water communications reported to lead from Slave Lake to the Northern Ocean. If I could not return and take charge of his department in his absence, he must abandon his intentions. Considering his regret at my refusal and the great importance of the object he had in view, I immediately set to work and accompanied him into Athabasca." Roderick was himself very likely persuaded by the partners' definite confirmation of the scheme and perhaps by the promise of a future N.W.Co. share.

Pond, according to Roderick's own *Reminiscences*, left Athabasca because, "being accused of the death of two gentlemen who were in opposition to his interest, he was now on his way out of the country on his defense." That may have been a way of getting rid of him, but no evidence has been found of any trial or enquiry during 1788 or 1789.

Pond may have sought legal advice. In late 1789 a young Quebec law clerk learned from conversation with the veteran trader that "as there is no other known Vent for the River setting out of Slave Lake, nor any other River in that Country to the Northward or Southward of Slave Lake to form such a River as Cook's River, there can be no doubt but the Source of Cook's River is now fully discovered and known. Another man by the name of McKenzie was left by Pond at Slave Lake to go down the River and from thence to Unalaska and so to Kamshatsha and thence to England through Russia." Those were great expectations.

Pond's discoveries and hopeful guesses; a profitable, land-based Pacific otter trade; Hudson's Bay Company plans for expansion and exploration; the chance of outstripping American and Russian merchants in occupying the Pacific Coast; Mackenzie's own strong personal ambitions as a trader and company man, and his more recently acquired appetite for exploration—all these pressures were urging the North West Company and its youngest partner towards a grand Pacific-seeking journey.

Mackenzie's ambitions were not riveted solely on exploration. He was a district trade manager, a partner, who had company work to do. This is where Roderick gave him so much help.

Back at Pond's fort in the late fall of 1788, he began to make alterations in the Athabasca department. The first change was in the site of the area's central post. Headquarters were moved from the river to the southern shore of Lake Athabasca. The Hudson's Bay Company men, Malcolm Ross and Turnor, who visited it in the summer of 1791 and wintered nearby, said it was about ten miles east of the mouth of the Athabasca River on a high, cleared sandy point with deep bays on either side that "nearly makes it an island." Roderick superintended its building. The name of the new house was Fort Chepewyan.

The main reason for the shift in location was to obtain a year-round supply of fish. Ninety to a hundred voyageurs fed and wintered here and their "whole dependence was on the lake and fishing implements." They lived "year after year, entirely upon fish, without even the quickening flavour of salt or vegetable." Mostly whitefish, perch and pike, which "about the setting of the hard frost crowd in shoals to the shallow water," were caught.

Nets, 360 feet long and six feet deep, were used and setting them in winter sometimes required chopping holes through five feet of ice. Working with the nets, hands were always kept immersed in the water. It was nearly freezing, but still a lot warmer than the surrounding air. According to Turnor, from nets set during the early winter spawning run, "as many fish may be taken as would serve four months." And fish "preserved by the frost have been found as sweet" in April "as when they were caught"—an early and unnoticed discovery of fresh-frozen food.

Of Lake Athabasca, Turnor wrote: "This lake is an exceeding fine place for Geese in the fall of the year at which time great numbers are then killed at the rate of two or three a shot." After a long dependence on fish, "fowl were a very gratifying food." Near the southern end of Slave River the Indians collected salt which they brought in great quantities to sell to Fort Chepewyan. It was used to preserve buffalo meat mostly.

From the plains around the subsidiary Peace River posts, freighted two tons at a time by three canoemen who did nothing else all summer, came pemmican. Mackenzie described its preparation:

The lean parts of the flesh of the larger animals are cut in thin slices and placed on a wooden grate over a slow fire, or exposed to the sun, and sometimes to the frost. These operations dry it. Then it is pounded between two stones. The inside fat and that of the rump is melted down and mixed in a boiling state with the pounded meat—in equal proportions. It is then put in baskets or bags for the convenience of carrying. A nutritious food, it is eaten without further preparation or addition of spice, salt, or vegetable. There is another sort made with the addition of marrow and dried berries which is of superior quality.

This food, which would "keep for several years," was the staple of the canoe brigades. They had to travel so hurriedly to and from Grand Portage that it was impossible to live off the land on the way. The canoes were serviced by pemmican depots at Fort Cumberland on the Saskatchewan and Fort Alexander on the Winnipeg. Rainy River was a country of wild rice, and good for food growing.

Turnor was greatly impressed by Fort Chepewyan. "I think this is the compleatest Inland House I have seen in the Country. This is the Grand Magazine of the Athapiscow Country and I am informed they have a sufficient quantity of Trading Goods in this country for at least two years to come." He noted that there was a plentiful supply of "Birch rind fitt for building large Canoes."

Concerning the birch tree and its bark, David Thompson said in his journals:

The White Birch is seldom more than four feet in circumference. A well grown tree will give from fifteen to thirty feet of Birch Rind. It requires a practised Man to raise it without injuring it. The best time for raising the rind off the Birch Tree is the early part of the summer. The tree being smooth is difficult to ascend, and for this purpose the Native ties a strong leather cord to the great toes of his feet, leaving a space between them of about foot. Having a strong square headed knife, very sharp at the point, in his belt, he ascends the tree to as high as the Rind is good.

He cuts downward in a straight line through the rind. While the sap is rising, the bark comes off so freely that two persons with light poles keep it to the trees until it can be carefully taken down. Then it is warmed and its circular form made flat, laid on the ground and kept so by light logs of wood. Thus it becomes fit for use. The common length from one tree is from nine to fifteen feet with a breadth of twenty four to thirty inches.

As the Birch Rind is impervious to water; Canoes are made of it.

A canoe of such stuff Mackenzie had ready for travel by early summer, 1789. On May 22, he wrote from Athabasca to the agents of the North West Company at Grand Portage: "Mr. Leroux arrived on the 22nd March from the north side of Slave Lake where he had seen a great number of Red Knives and Slave Indians. They traded with him and promised to meet him this summer. I intend to pass that way on my voyage for a supply of provisions."

He left twelve days later.

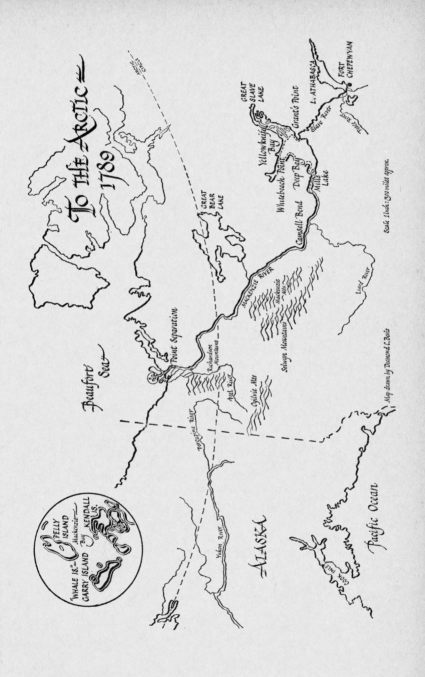

Chapter four

In search of Cook's river

"JUNE, 1789. WEDNESDAY, 3—We embarked at nine in the morning at Fort Chepewyan in a canoe made of birch bark." Its crew consisted of a German called John Steinbruck and four Canadians: François Barrieau, Charles Ducette, Joseph Landry, and Pierre de Lorme. Two of the Canadians had their wives with them.

An Indian known as the English Chief, because he had often led trading bands along the Churchill to the English posts on Hudson Bay, was also a member of the exploring party. He was accompanied in a small canoe by his two wives. In another small canoe were two young Indians, his followers. "These men were engaged to serve us in the two-fold capacity of interpreters and hunters."

Mackenzie's canoe carried provisions of pemmican and corn, "the clothing necessary for us on the voyage, a proper assortment of merchandise as presents to ensure us a friendly reception among the Indians," arms and ammunition for hunting—and, if need be, for defence.

Their firearms were muzzle-loading flintlock muskets, basically the same weapon, although lighter, that won for Wolfe his victory at Quebec. In the fur trade the light musket was known as the "North West gun" or "Hudson's Bay fuke." Mackenzie gave his firearms several names: muskets, fowling-pieces, or "fusees," an English phonetic spelling of the French word for guns, *fusils*.

With a barrel length of three to four feet, the trade gun was made light enough that it could be carried all day easily. Unrifled, accurate only up to about sixty yards, its smooth bore permitted the use of shot or ball in any length of barrel, but the longer barrel made the better fowling-piece or bird-gun; the short barrel was a buffalo-hunt weapon. From bar lead, melted and poured into moulds, shot or ball could be quickly prepared. Powder, a factory-made mixture of about three-quarters saltpetre and an eighth each of charcoal and sulphur, was carried in a canister, flask, or home-made powder horn.

Used by a skilful, patient hunter, the trade gun was an effective hunting tool; carried by every man on Mackenzie's expedition, it was their passport to security.

From Fort Chepewyan—its present-day spelling and location both changed—Mackenzie's small brigade went north on the Slave River. Company canoes had been up and down the stream many times and the portage trails had long been blazed, so the river held no surprises. The travellers experienced those minor hazards familiar to all who paddled the watery highways of the Northwest and tented on their banks. A canoe was lost when the current caught and hurled it over some falls. The only occupant, an Indian woman, scrambled out in the nick of time and got safely ashore.

They endured also, almost as an unnoticed part of their working lives, the wilderness discomforts: the grunting portage chores, drumming showers and soaking rain, blustery winds and cold. A man could find some escape from chill and damp beside a fire or under canvas; there was none from the tormenting clouds of insects. They attacked in hordes along the carrying paths, hovered in whining swarms over the evening camps, and their crazed chorus filled the tents. For a whole week, there was no relief from their maddening bites.

Then the river opened onto Slave Lake. They turned east. Protected by a long sand bar, they paddled to Grant's Point. Wind-driven ice blocked the way north.

As well as they could, here and during the whole trip, they lived off the country, "as it was absolutely necessary that the stores provided for our future voyage should remain untouched." Nets set for fish yielded carp, pike, whitefish, trout, *poisson inconnu*—related to the common whitefish; the hunters stalked deer, swans, geese, beaver; the women gathered berries and duck's eggs. Although guns and nets were not always productive, the pemmican and corn supply was saved as a last-resort ration for the days when hunting and fishing might not be successful, or when the expedition might have to devote all its time to hurried or laboured travel. And such days were to come.

Not until the fifteenth of the month did the expedition strike camp. The lake was clogged with stampeding ice floes, charging back and forth before wild winds. Cautiously the canoes fled from island to island as passages were swept clear by a stiff breeze. The forty-mile northern crossing took six days.

"We pitched our tents on one of a cluster of small islands within three miles of the main land, which we could not reach because of the ice. We saw some rein-deer and our hunters went in pursuit. They killed five large and two small ones." In celebration of the feast, the island was named *Isle de Carreboeuf*—probably by a hungry and grateful Canadian. The name stuck; and the whole group is today called the Caribou Islands.

Mackenzie entered the long northern arm of Slave Lake and continued his journey across the yawning mouth of Yellowknife Bay to Leroux's trading station opposite Whitebeach Point. "We landed at three lodges of Red Knife Indians, so called from their copper knives." One of the Indians was sent to fetch companions camped not far away and then meeting all in impressive assembly, Mackenzie told them: "If they brought a sufficient quantity of skins, the Canadians would return for more goods to winter, and build a fort."

This business done, on Thursday June 25, with a Red Knife Indian to guide them to the river draining Slave Lake, Mackenzie left Leroux behind to reap the packages of fur. "We were saluted on our departure with some volleys of small arms, which we returned."

The volleying guns announced the true beginning of the voyage. Ahead of them was unknown country, threaded only by small roving bands of hunters and fishermen, themselves acquainted with but a fraction of the vast wilderness. The lake's northern arm, only a few miles wide here, was crossed, and the canoes pointed south, hugging the shore. Two days later the birch-bark craft bumped into a heavy swell on the main body of the lake.

The search for the lake's broad exit started. It was somewhere to the west, at the end of a long funnelling bay, where the looming cumulus sat on a water-rimmed horizon. Led by the guide, the tiny fleet glided from point to jutting point, sliding past scores of inlets and when the lake grew rough and dangerous, scurrying to camp on shore. Whenever they landed, grey partridges shot skywards everywhere in explosive greeting and the ground was pitted with the tracks of caribou and moose.

Eventually they came "to the point of a very deep bay," ten miles wide, but its end they could not see. As well as the guide was able to remember, "this bay appeared to be the entrance to the river." They steered down it, and were met by menacing white squadrons of ice which challenged their advance and surrounded the canoes. Then layers of curling fog enveloped them. Warding off the jagged phalanx of ice with the paddles, they retreated and luckily found, just before sunset, protection on a small island.

Sure that no current ran into the bay, Mackenzie next morning set course for the southern point and rounded it. After midday, the coast-line bent and thinned into the northwest, its narrow shaft piercing the far horizon. Mackenzie stared out over the huge basin. Maybe the lake's draining river was there.

The mast was raised and only three feet of sail spread to catch a strong wind blowing right into the bay. The canoe jumped forward. Sometimes for a few thrilling seconds they surfed before the crest of a great heaving wave, the helmsman straining to hold the stern steady. Then the craft yawed, lost momentum, and the wave washed past spilling over all along the gunwales. Down and back the craft dropped, slipped, slowed; the sail bulging, ballooning, nearly bursting with wind, until an oncoming wave hoisted them up again.

All the time while the canoe was lifting and speeding, falling and stalling, a man bailed hard with the kettle. Faintly the distant shore-line was seen; but whether the waters crashed on sand, rock or reeds they could not tell. They closed nearer and saw the waves rolling into shallows strewn with rushes. The canoe slithered into the bottom of the bay.

Twice wrong now, the guide was not very popular. The English Chief, who arrived two or three hours later, a bit worn and somewhat frightened by paddling on the rough lake, made loud angry sounds and said he would kill him for his ignorance. But the Red Knife had actually got his bearings at last and told Mackenzie that he remembered crossing overland to their present camp from the river.

On modern maps the place is named Deep Bay.

"Monday, June 29.—We embarked at four this morning, and steered along the South-West side of the bay. At half past five we reached the extremity of the point, which we doubled, and found it to be the branch or passage that was the object of our search."

Mackenzie was jubilant. They struck out into the stream and joined its westerly course for Cook's Inlet and the Pacific. Gradually the river narrowed from ten miles to half a mile wide where the current swiftened. A sail-stretching breeze sped them between greening islands and past yellow clay banks topped by fire-burnt woods.

Fifty to sixty miles downstream, the river widened, the wind died down and the canoes thrust forward under paddle. "We could not discover an opening in any direction as our Red-Knife Indian had never explored beyond here." Only occasionally did his people come this far to hunt moose and the wood buffalo. Mackenzie followed the north shore, got into reeds, recovered deep water, and paddled round southward to where the channel of the river opened again. Here they camped soon after sunset and supped on two geese and a swan killed by the hunters. They had circled Mills Lake.

From this place the river hastened westerly. The voyageurs, running with the stream, brimful of energy and strength, surely chanted their paddle songs in joyful overture to the great river's promise.

Although it was July, there were still "quantities of ice along the banks." They saw a few signs of human life: "a white goose, which appeared to have been lately shot with an arrow and was quite fresh"; on a small island, poles of four lodges, "which belonged to the Knisteneaux [Cree], on their war excursions, six or seven years ago"; two Indian encampments of the last year, where Mackenzie with a trader's eye guessed that "by the manner in which these people cut their wood, they have no iron tools."

Most of the daylight hours were spent on the river if the weather was fair. Usually the party embarked about four in the morning, rarely later and often earlier, and went on shore for the night about eight. The pace was not leisurely. "The Indians complained of the perseverance with which we pushed forward, and that they were not accustomed to such fatigue as it occasioned."

The current rushed so powerfully along this section of the river that when Mackenzie's sounding line snagged in the river bottom, eight men were not able to back the canoe up to release it. The line itself Mackenzie estimated equal to the strength of four paddles. No wonder then that everyone was alert for "The Great Waterfall" shown on Pond's map.

"We continually expected to approach some great rapid or fall. All of us were occasionally persuaded that we heard those sounds which betokened a fall of water." One afternoon, the current was so strong "that it was in actual ebullition, and produced a hissing noise like a kettle of water in a moderate state of boiling."

On July 2, at nine in the morning, "we saw a very high mountain ahead, which appeared on our nearer approach to be a cluster of mountains stretching as far as our view could reach to the Southward, and whose tops were lost in the clouds. They appeared also to be sprinkled with white stones which glistened in the sun and which were called by the Indians *manetoe aseniah*, or spirit stones. On our return, however, these appearances were dissolved, as they were nothing more than patches of snow."

When the canoes neared the base of the mountains, the river did not plunge through them to the Pacific. Instead, its western rush was checked by the mountain wall, and it swung sharply to the right. Dourly, Mackenzie observed the dramatic right-angle turn in the river. Perhaps it would regain its westerly course at the next bend.

Whatever happened, he was committed to the river taking him where it would. He had to keep going; the company's partners would scorn anything less than a report on the whole river. And he himself would not be satisfied unless he witnessed its end. After all, no one had been this way before; there were discoveries to be made. According to Pond, the coast was not very far west of Fort Chepewyan. Maybe some people on the banks of this river could guide him to the northern Pacific.

Day after day, as the canoes were borne northward now, he scanned the river banks for signs of human habitation.

Chapter five

Across the Circle

O<small>N SUNDAY JULY</small> 5, "the sun rose at seven minutes before two: we embarked soon after. At three-quarters past seven o'clock, we saw several smokes on the North shore."

As we drew nearer, we noticed the natives running about in great confusion. Some were making to the woods, and others were hurrying to their canoes. Our hunters landed before us, and in the Chepewyan language addressed the few that had not escaped. So great was their confusion and terror, they did not appear to understand. But when they saw that it was impossible to avoid us as we were all landed, they made us signs to keep at a distance. We obeyed, and not only unloaded our canoe but pitched our tents before we made any attempt to approach them.

There were five families, consisting of twenty-five or thirty persons, and of two different tribes, the Slave and Dog-rib Indians. We made them smoke though they did not know the use of tobacco; we likewise supplied them with grog. We got more influence over them by the distribution of knives, beads, awls, rings, gartering, fire-steels, flints, and hatchets, so that they became more familiar even than we expected; for we could not keep them out of our tents.

Mackenzie thought them "a meagre, ugly, ill-made people," unhealthy, covered with dirt and grease, their legs scabby, their hair long and unkempt.

The men have two double lines, either black or blue, tattooed upon each cheek, from the ear to the nose. The gristle of the latter is perforated so as to admit a goose-quill or a small piece of wood.

During our short stay with these people, they amused us with dancing. The men leap about and occasionally howl in imitation of some animal. He who continues this exercise longest appears to be considered as the best performer.

Their weapons and tools he described in some detail:

The pogamagon is made of the horn of the rein-deer, the branches being all cut off, except one at the end. This instrument is about two feet in length, and is used to kill their enemies in battle, and such animals as they catch in snares.

Their axes are manufactured of a piece of brown or grey stone from six to eight inches long and two inches thick. The inside is flat, and the outside round and tapering to an edge an inch wide. They are fastened by the middle with the flat side inwards to a handle two feet long, with a cord of green skin. This is the tool with which they split their wood.

"They kindle fire by striking a piece of pyrites and flint stone over touchwood." These fire-making materials, with drills of horn and knives of beaver teeth, were carried in a bag and sheath hung around the neck.

From these people Mackenzie learned "that it would require several winters to get to the sea and that old age would come upon us before our return. We were also to encounter monsters of horrid shapes and destructive powers. They added that there were two impassable falls in the river; the first was about thirty days' march."

Whether this is what they really said Mackenzie had no way of knowing. He had to take the word of his interpreters, "who were already tired of the voyage" and wanted to quit. "According to the information which they had received, there were very few animals in the country beyond us. As we proceeded the scarcity would increase and we should perish from hunger."

Mackenzie scoffed at all this primitive nonsense and persuaded "one of those Indians to guide us, in exchange for a small kettle, an axe, a knife, and some other articles."

Just before leaving, the guide "cut off a lock of his hair and divided it into three parts. He fastened one of them to the hair on his wife's head, blowing on it three times with the utmost violence in his power and uttering certain words. The other two he fastened, with the same formalities, on the heads of his two children."

They shoved off. "We soon passed the Great-Bear-Lake River, which is of considerable depth, and a hundred yards wide: its water is clear and has the greenish hue of the sea." Six miles downstream, gusting winds and pelting rain forced the canoes off the river. Camp was made at the foot of a rocky hill. Already the Dog-rib was homesick and begged to return. "It was necessary to keep a strict watch over him during the night."

For five more days the canoes dropped downriver. Just above the present site of Fort Good Hope, they twisted seven miles through the white-walled channel of the Ramparts, rising two hundred feet straight out of the water. Again and again Mackenzie stopped at Indian camps to exchange presents of ironware for food or for information about the river, to win friends and to prepare the way for future trade, but mostly to bargain for a guide.

The river-bank residents were nearly always fearful. At one stopping-place everybody scampered into the woods except an old man who "did not hesitate to approach us. He represented himself as too far advanced in life, and too indifferent about the short time he had to remain in the world to be very anxious about escaping from any danger that threatened him. At the same time he pulled his grey hairs from his head by handfuls to distribute among us and implored our favour for himself and his relations."

They purchased fish, hares and partridges, and refused from some Indians returning from a hunting foray the offer of caribou meat which "was rotten, as well as offensive to the smell." Guides were less easily bought than food or dubious information about "a *Manitoe* or spirit in the river which swallowed every person that approached it," about the distance to the sea, or about the "Esquimaux, a very wicked people, who would put us all to death."

Eventually, however, the Dog-rib guide was released and hurried happily home to his wife and children. His successor deserted during a thunderous and rainy night, but a luckless companion who had followed the expedition was pressed into service in his place. No more willing to remain with it than the others, he was kept in tow by compulsion and constant watching until an exchange was found for him among a tribe called the Hare Indians.

Early on the morning of the tenth of July, the canoes were paddled beneath the three-hundred-foot cliffs of the Lower Ramparts, and on passing through them, crossed the Arctic Circle. In front were the snow-peaked Richardson Mountains, the same range that had forced the river north.

Ten miles below the Lower Ramparts, "the river widens and runs through islands, some of which are little more than banks of mud and sand. Others are covered with a kind of spruce fir. So various were the channels that we were at a loss which to take."

They had to come to Point Separation and were looking on the delta of the great river. Its terminus, where it emptied its vast volume of waters, was within reach.

"I determined to take the middle channel as it appeared to be a larger body of water running North and South."

Chapter six

To the edge of the ice

Nᴏᴛ ꜰᴀʀ ᴘᴀꜱᴛ Point Separation, Mackenzie "obtained an observation that gave me 67.47 North latitude." This was "further North than I expected."

The main reason why Mackenzie believed himself not so far north is that he underestimated the distances he had travelled—and the directions, too. From Slave Lake to Point Separation he logged 629 miles. The actual distance is about 860; so, he was short by roughly twenty miles a day—a pretty large error in an average daily run of seventy-five miles. Also, the canoes had in fact been pointing more northerly than the directions he took from his compass.

Anyway, when he stopped in the delta to observe the sun and calculate his latitude—the first time in a week that he was able to see the noon sun to do so—he knew for sure that he was inside the Arctic Circle. Day after day he had probably put aside the unwelcome fact of the river's northern swing. After all, it need not deny his hopes, and they were made of durable stuff. The Indian accounts of the Eskimos was information harder to suppress. But now the evidence of sun and sextant must have washed over him like a cold, choking wave of disappointment; for he could not possibly be on Cook's River or any of its branches.

Still, even if he had to winter far from the friendly comforts of Fort Chepewyan, Mackenzie was determined to go as far as the mouth of the river because, as his manuscript journal says, "it would satisfy Peoples Curiosity tho' not their Intentions." His Indian employees were not so keen; "they would have left me if it had been in their power." Their co-operation was retained by the promise "that I would proceed onwards but seven days more and if I did not then get to the sea, I would return." In any event it was a promise made necessary "by the low state of our provisions." He also judged it politic to buy their reluctant support; the guide's with the gift of a dressed moose-skin, "a valuable present," and the English Chief's with one of Mackenzie's travelling coats, a *capote* or what we would call a parka.

Mackenzie marked his arrival inside the Arctic by sitting up all night to observe the sun. "At half past twelve I called up one of the men to view a spectacle which he had never before seen. Seeing the sun so high, he thought it was a signal to embark and began to call the rest of his companions. They could hardly be persuaded that it was but a short time past midnight."

The channel coiled snakelike through the low-lying islands and, as they paused to camp and eat along its serpentine path, they noticed signs of Eskimo. At one spot Mackenzie "counted thirty places where there had been fires; and some of the men who went further saw as many more." There were poles fixed in the river for holding fish nets, scattered pieces of whalebone, spilled train or whale oil, and parts of canoe frames. In the early afternoon of the eleventh, the expedition left the broad path of the middle channel and nosed northward through the delta maze.

Here they saw more traces of Eskimo. There were huts with a floor space of fifteen by ten feet and lined with split wood. Half of this area was dug twelve inches below ground level and covered with willow branches, "which probably serves as a bed for the whole family." Part of the remaining floor area was dug two feet below the ground, "the only spot in the house where a grown person can stand upright." Mackenzie guessed this was the hearth or fireplace.

The door or entrance is in the middle of one end of the house and is about two feet and an half high, and two feet wide. It has a covered way or porch five feet in length so that it is absolutely necessary to creep on all fours to get into or out of this curious habitation. There is a hole of about eighteen inches square on the top of it which serves the threefold purpose of a window, an occasional door, and a chimney.

Six or eight stumps of small trees driven into the earth with the root upwards, on which are laid some cross pieces of timber, support the roof of the building which is an oblong square of ten feet by six. The whole is made of drift-wood covered with branches and dry-grass over which is laid a foot deep of earth. In and about the houses we found sledge runners, pieces of whalebone, and poplar bark cut in circles which are used as corks to buoy the nets.

We expected through the day to meet some of the natives. On several of the islands we noticed the print of their feet in the sand as if they had been there but a few days before to procure wild fowl.

Mackenzie made sure that the firearms were in order.

According to the guide, "we were to see a larger lake on the morrow. The Esquimaux alone inhabit its shores, and kill a large fish that is found in it and which is a principal part of their food. He also mentioned white bears and another large animal which was seen in those parts, but our hunters could not understand the description which he gave of it." Perhaps it was the musk-ox.

Camp was made at eight. It was cold and rained all through the night. Next morning, Sunday July 12, the canoes meandered through "country so naked that scarce a shrub was to be seen." Short grass and flowers covered the high land "though the earth was not thawed above four inches" over solid ice, and the low land was still blanketed with ice and snow. "The soil, where there is any, is a yellow clay mixed with stones."

Eskimo remains were still abundant—more huts, sledge bars and runners, small pieces of flint fixed into handles of wood, wooden dishes, parts of a large canoe, and pieces of netting made of sinews. The netting was plaited or braided, "and no ordinary portion of time must have been employed in manufacturing so great a length of cord. A square stone-kettle with a flat bottom also occupied our attention. It was capable of containing two gallons and we were puzzled as to the means these people must have used to chisel it out of a solid rock into its present form." All these things were left as if the owners might return at any moment; and, during their furtive, fascinated inspection, the travellers were perhaps not without strange, creeping fears that from somewhere there might suddenly come an angry, yelling crowd to dispute their presence.

When they embarked, the stream traced a wandering but strong course. The guide, who "seemed to be as ignorant of this country as ourselves," was of no help. They were lost, a silent circle of sky all round, in a desolate labyrinth of islands and channels.

Then the exit from the island tangle turned west and straightway opened, and before them they saw its shore arms spreading wider and wider to embrace a broadening, unbroken horizon. It was the sea and their journey's end. Resting their paddles across the gunwales, they let the current carry them to a high hummock eight miles ahead. Here they beached the canoes and Mackenzie squinted through the sextant sights at the noon sun. They were on the very edge of the delta.

"The lake was quite open to the Westward." There the top of an island was visible, the only land in sight. The day was clear and windless. It was a temptation too great for Mackenzie's adventurous spirit. The canoes were ordered onto the water.

At five o'clock we arrived at the island, landed, and as soon as the tents were pitched, I proceeded with the English Chief to the highest part of the island. We discovered the solid ice extending from the South-West by compass to the Eastward. We could dimly make out a chain of mountains at the distance of upwards of twenty leagues stretching further to the North than the edge of the ice. To the Eastward we saw many islands.

Mackenzie had reached an island beyond the delta shore, climbed a high hill, and surveyed the landless, ice-covered western Arctic Ocean. He was the first European to do so.

The Canadians expressed genuine disappointment that they had not reached the Pacific. Their spirits had been raised by the hopes "that another day would bring them to the *Mer d'Ouest*. Even in our present situation they declared their readiness to follow me wherever I should be pleased to lead them." That was a magnificent declaration of loyalty. One wonders whether Mackenzie had spoken around the evening campfire of coasting westward along the Arctic shore. He didn't know it, but Bering Strait was a thousand miles to the west around Point Barrow and Cape Lisburne, and Cook's Inlet two thousand miles of coast-line beyond the strait.

Monday was a deserved sabbatical from toil. In the afternoon Mackenzie climbed the island's hill again, and noted that a hard-blowing west wind had not set the ice in motion. The nets yielded only a couple of edible fish about the size of a herring. Food was a problem, "our stores being reduced to about five hundred weight which would not have lasted fifteen people more than twelve days."

About eight the next morning one of the men was startled to see the ice moving and bobbing about. Mackenzie was called to have a look. "They were whales." Again he gave in to an impulsive, adventure-seeking curiosity. "I ordered the canoe to be prepared and we embarked in pursuit of them. It was a wild and unreflecting enterprise, and it was fortunate that we failed to overtake them. A stroke from the tail of one of these enormous fish would have dashed the canoe to pieces. Our guide informed us that they are frequently seen as large as our canoe. The part of them which appeared above the water was altogether white." Before they got too close to the creatures, fog sent the canoe skeltering back to the island.

About noon the fog lifted and Mackenzie ordered the canoe into the water once more, "being curious to take a view of the ice." An hour later the fog swirled back, blotting out the ice and dimming the outline of the island. Then the wind leapt suddenly out of the northeast. The sail was hoisted and, with two men bailing furiously, a tight tack was set through the rising swell for the blurred silhouette of the island. They made it, although the Indians in their smaller canoes very nearly didn't.

Later in the day, camp was shifted to "the Eastern end of the island, which I had named the Whale Island." (This was probably what is now called Garry Island.) The wind, still blowing hard, and Mackenzie's desire to observe whether there was a tide, kept the expedition inactive here another day. By then Mackenzie's earlier promise to return in seven days fell due.

So, the delta was re-entered, the canoes "stemmed the current," and the frozen sea was left astern. On Whale Island on the morning of the fourteenth, Mackenzie had "ordered a post to be erected close to our tents, on which I engraved the latitude of the place, my own name, the number of persons which I had with me, and the time we remained there."

It was a record which unfortunately could not have survived many arctic winters.

Chapter seven

By paddle, sail and towing-line

W HEN MACKENZIE "made for the river, and stemmed the current," it was with the hope of meeting the Eskimos. Perhaps it was just as well that he didn't; ten years later a five-man Arctic exploring party under the North West Company trader Duncan Livingstone, the first to follow Mackenzie's trail, was wiped out by those people.

Back on the river, the temperature was warmer, so they were again "subjected to the persecution of the mosquitoes," but the biggest worry was getting enough to eat. The evening nets caught few fish and the only success achieved by the Indian hunters in two days' foraging was three geese, two cranes, a white owl, and some caribou tracks. So, the provisions had to be broached, and though the pemmican had been mouldy for some time, it satisfied their ravenous appetites.

In a couple of days the situation improved. The hunters shot two caribou, and cranberries were plentiful in certain low spots near the river. One afternoon the Indians killed eight geese. Next day they shot twenty-two, and the day after, "we saw great numbers of fowl and killed among us fifteen geese and four swans."

It took five days for the canoes to make their way back through the delta to Point Separation. In the mainstream the current was so strong that travel by paddle was too exhausting. The 360-foot towing-line was used to pull the canoe; it was tough work too. The banks were high and almost perpendicular; the shore-line was narrow and covered with a grey stone that occasionally showered down on the men from the precipices above.

"The men in the canoe relieved two of those on shore every two hours." They camped just above the Lower Ramparts.

Within an hour some Indians, among them the brother of their guide who had recently deserted, arrived. They were suspicious of Mackenzie's account of the guide's escape; but the brother "nevertheless proposed for a small quantity of beads to believe everything I should say. I contented myself with giving him the bow and arrows which our conductor had left with us."

They might have been troublesome had they not been scared some days before by the volleying blast of the guns when the expedition embarked from their camp for the Arctic with the guide. So, when the party began putting their firearms in order after the previous day's rain, the river natives were frightened. They were assured that the preparations were for hunting and that there was no intention to hurt them.

"All my people went to rest; but I thought it prudent to sit up in order to watch the natives." They asked why he didn't sleep like the others, and "their curiosity was still more excited when they saw me writing." After midnight, and after being driven away from the bubbling food kettles, the visitors "kindled a small fire, and laid themselves down to sleep round it like so many whelps, having neither skins nor garments of any kind to cover them, notwithstanding the cold."

On the following day, the canoe was towed from half past three in the morning until eight in the evening "except two hours when we employed the sail." For the first three hours of the day Mackenzie walked with the Indians to their dwellings.

They had large huts built with driftwood on the slope of the beach and inside the earth was dug away to form a level floor. At each end was a stout fork whereon was laid a strong ridge-pole which formed a support to the whole structure. A covering of spruce bark preserved it from the rain.

Spars of different heights were fixed within the hut and covered with split fish that hung on them to dry. Fires were made to quicken the operation. There were rails also on the outside of the building which were hung around with fish, but fresher than those inside. We obtained as many fish as the canoe would conveniently contain, and some strings of beads were the price paid for them, an article which they preferred to every other. Iron they held in little or no estimation.

All the next day, for fifteen hours, the men trudged along a narrow stony beach, fighting the current step by step, the line tautening as they pulled and tugged. Footsore, they slept, and woke to haul again. Near noon a spanking breeze blew south. The marching voyageurs slipped the tow-line from their shoulders and took their places in the canoe. The sail was raised, the paddles bit into the water and the prow parted the current.

At twelve, sail up, the canoe was steered towards an Indian lodge on the riverside. Three men, who had retreated some distance from the camp, waited with bows and arrows at the ready and twanged a warning thrum on the bowstrings. Holding out a present of beads, Mackenzie approached slowly and carefully.

What had alarmed them was the sail. It was not an Indian technique and so Mackenzie's party had been taken for Eskimos. They remained hostile; none of the others returned from the woods. Since they had no food to barter, Mackenzie ordered the canoe under way.

For a few days they worked upstream by paddle, dipping powerfully, endlessly, hour after hour on their knees, stroking in unison a steady, rhythmic hymn to endurance. Early on the morning of the twenty-sixth they landed and woke the slumbering inhabitants of three large huts. Among these people was a Dog-rib man whose language the English Chief understood well.

They spoke, and Mackenzie was told by his interpreter "that there is a river on the other side of the mountains to the South-West which falls into the *Belhoullay Teo* or White-man's Lake." Compared to it the river they were on was but a small stream. The Dog-rib reported "that the natives were very large, and very wicked, and kill common people with their eyes; that those who inhabit the entrance of it kill a kind of beaver whose skin is almost red; and that large canoes often frequent it. As there is no known communication by water with this river, the natives who saw it went over the mountains."

The story was vague and fanciful, but it suggested that perhaps Cook's River could be reached after all. Hopes refreshened, Mackenzie now wanted to find out everything he could about this Pacific-flowing river on the other side of the mountains.

On the succeeding day he revisited another Indian camp near the site of Fort Good Hope. A gift of beads persuaded one fellow to draw a map of the surrounding country on the sand. "I made an advantageous proposition to this man to accompany me across the mountains to the other river, but he refused it." It was a bold proposal. The nearest westward-flowing streams were tributaries of the Yukon, two hundred miles southwest through rugged mountainous country. What a journey, tale, and extension of empire that would have been!

Told that a short piece upriver there were people who had just recently come down from the western mountains to fish, and that these people were the best qualified to help him find "the other river," Mackenzie set off to contact them. He reached their camp at ten and instructed his followers to get ready to spend the rest of the day here. At four in the afternoon, when he judged the Indians might be relaxed and talkative, he ordered his interpreter to begin his interrogation.

Their account of the river to the Westward was similar to that already received: and they represented the inhabitants as being of gigantic stature and adorned with wings which they never employed in flying. They described the people that inhabited the mouth of the river as possessing the extraordinary power of killing with their eyes, and devouring a large beaver at a single meal. Canoes of very large dimensions visited that place.

They did not relate these strange circumstances from their own knowledge, but on the reports of other tribes; for they themselves never ventured beyond the first mountains where they went in search of the small white buffaloes. The inhabitants of the other side kill them whenever they meet.

This weird, distorted account of the ships and traders on the Pacific coast was naturally discounted by Mackenzie, but he did not try to translate its oddities.

The "wings" could be capes, coats, or sails, or sheer fancy; "killing with their eyes" might be nothing more than sighting down a gun barrel; the "white buffaloes" were mountain sheep.

Mackenzie suspected that the English Chief, "who had long been tired of the voyage," might keep to himself any information that would encourage a continued search for Cook's River. So, after the Indians had danced themselves into exhaustion, an "exercise accompanied by loud imitations of the noises produced by the rein-deer, the bear, and the wolf," he had the English Chief renew enquiries about the land westward, "which he did without success."

I therefore assumed an angry air, expressed my suspicions that they withheld their information, and concluded with a menace that if they did not give me all the satisfaction in their power, I would force one of them along with me to-morrow to point out the other river. On this declaration, they all at one and the same moment became sick, and answered in a very faint tone that they knew no more than they had already communicated, and that they would die if I took any of them away.

Mackenzie did not press the point; he purchased some fish and left. He did not see any more Indians to question about the river west of the mountains.

For nearly two weeks he pushed relentlessly upriver, sometimes leaving the hunters sulking far behind. Past rapids or a current rolling too swiftly to be conquered by paddle, the men towed. Stony beaches bruised their feet cruelly. "The women, who did not quit the canoe, were continually employed in making shoes of mooseskin for the men as a pair did not last more than a day."

A walk along the bank, near the Great Bear River for example, could be interesting—for Mackenzie. There were springs of mineral water, lumps of iron ore, and along one stretch "the whole bank was on fire for a very considerable distance. It proved to be a coal mine to which the fire had communicated from an old Indian encampment."

On they went. Occasionally an aft wind was sail-harnessed in the upstream struggle. In eddy currents near the shore, where the giant strength of the river did not grasp and grab at the canoe, the men bent to the paddles. They made their panting, sweating way beneath the monstrous face of the Ramparts, past lofty mud banks still plated with ice, over shoals of sand and pebbles—for the water had fallen five feet or more since their descent.

They travelled through unbearable heat, and then suddenly gusting down from the Arctic came winds so cold that, even with their perspiring labours, they "could not put on clothes enough to keep warm." Twice, thunderstorms of demoniac fury lashed the evening tents; and once, "a hurricane threatened to carry away the canoe which had been fastened to some trees with a cod-line."

In these bitter daily trials they were sustained by geese from the hunters' guns, by ripening whortleberries, raspberries, and a berry called *poire*—"of purple hue, somewhat bigger than a pea, and of luscious taste"; on liquorice root, "of which there is a great abundance on the banks of the river"; and on the corn brought with them from Chepewyan. One reindeer was killed, "and from the wounds in her hind legs, it was supposed that she had been pursued by wolves who had devoured her young one. Her udder was full of milk and one of the young Indians poured it among some boiled corn which he ate with great delight, esteeming it a very delicious food."

Eventually, on Monday August 10, "we landed opposite to the mountains which we had passed on the second of the last month."

Their camp was near Camsell Bend, where the river had disappointingly bent north.

"As these mountains are the last of any magnitude on the South-West side of the river, I ordered my men to cross to that side so I might climb one of them." The Canadians were too worn with fatigue to share his curiosity. One of the young Indians volunteered to join him. For an hour they wormed their way through a thick underwood of spruce fir, came clear beneath tall, thrusting columns of white birch and poplar, and then pressed up a slope covered and scented with small pines. "At length we got the first view of the mountains since we had left the canoe. Though we had been walking for three hours, they appeared to be no nearer to us."

The Indian, his shoes and leggings ripped and torn by branches, pleaded with Mackenzie to go back. But even if it meant passing the night where they were, the stubborn young Scot had made up his mind to clamber up a peak; perhaps he thought to look out, like Balboa, upon the Pacific. The ground turned soggy and wet near the base of the mountains. They trudged and splashed to within a mile of them through water and grass knee-high. The marsh deepened a little; its bed softened. Suddenly Mackenzie sank into it, mired in the muck and water up to his armpits.

Somehow he got out. Maybe he had been frightened by his own foolhardiness. Anyway, he turned back through the darkening woods with his companion and arrived at the canoe by midnight.

With this unnerving experience, Mackenzie's search for a way to the Pacific was closed—for the year 1789.

Chapter eight

Homeward bound

THE NEXT TWELVE days were spent travelling from Camsell Bend to the entrance of Great Slave Lake. Until they came to the last few miles of the river, the current was moderate, their pace leisurely, and the strenuous labours of the line no longer necessary. There was a temporary respite from the cold; excepting one showery day, the weather was generally fine, even occasionally sultry. Fires were consuming the forests. As well there was a lull in the adventures of the voyage; but they were not over.

Mackenzie was still eager to learn more from local Indians about the land to the west. Unattended campfires were passed, although no natives were met; some were tracked, but without success. The one group who were seen dashed terror-stricken into the woods as the exploring party approached. Instead of chasing after them, the English Chief and his followers began looting and dividing their possessions. "I immediately ordered him, his young men, and my own people to go in search of the natives, but their fears had made them too nimble and we could not overtake them."

Mackenzie, by nature a patient and tolerant leader, lost his temper—partly because he suspected that the English Chief and the young hunters were afraid of being made to follow him if he should hear encouraging "accounts of the other river." Perhaps without realizing it, Mackenzie tried to find in anger a release from the disappointment of not reaching Cook's River.

Anyhow, he scolded the English Chief to tears and then let him wail and whine undisturbed for two hours. However, since his services were needed as a hunter, the Chief was invited to supper at Mackenzie's tent. A dram or two of rum and a few forgiving words from his employer soothed his sorrows. "He informed me that it was a custom with the Chepewyan chiefs to go to war after they had shed tears in order to wipe away the disgrace attached to such a feminine weakness." So, when spring came, he would don the war bonnet. "I took care that he should carry some liquid consolation to his lodges to prevent the return of his chagrin."

As always, their constant concern during these days was food. Unsuccessful, the hunters complained that "the woods were so thick that it was impossible to follow the game through them." They got only a beaver, a few hares, a couple of dozen geese, and a wolf, "which the men ate with great satisfaction." The nets were hauled up empty, but the women patiently picked cranberries, crowberries, gooseberries, *poires*, mooseberries, a few strawberries, and a fruit called *pathagomenan*. "Something like a raspberry," it was found "on a small stalk in wet, mossy spots."

When the expedition retrieved two bags of pemmican which, in order to lighten the deeply laden canoe, had been concealed on an island not far from "the river of the mountains" or the Liard River, the hunters rested while the men paddled unstintingly on. At Mills Lake, "the English Chief presented us with an eagle, three cranes, a small beaver, and two geese," which sounds like a truly northern meal.

The provisions of corn and pemmican, their last defence against starvation, were now nearly gone. Mackenzie equipped all the Indians for a hunt; that evening they fed on buffalo. While the Indians continued their search for game, the canoe was gummed and repaired, and new paddles carved to mount the last stretch of the river.

On Saturday August 22, "the wind veered round to the Westward and continued to blow strong and cold. We renewed our voyage and in three hours reached the entrance of the Slave Lake, under half sail. With paddle, it would have taken us at least eight hours. The wind was so violent that it was too risky to venture into the lake." The canoes entered the lake proper on Sunday. Mackenzie thought of following the south shore to the mouth of the Slave River; it was shorter. But the certain abundance of fish along the north shore made him prefer that route. Besides, Leroux had been commanded to wait for him in the north arm of the lake until the fall.

With favouring aft winds their sail-rigged craft scudded through the boisterous lake, the mast straining and the water often pouring in on both sides. Leroux, out on a hunting trip, was met and the two parties returned to his trading house.

The English Chief and the two young hunters followed as best they could over rough waters. Twice their canoe had broken on the swell and they had nearly perished before the waves washed them ashore. "I gave them a plentiful equipment of iron ware, ammunition, tobacco, &c., as a recompense for the toil and inconvenience they had sustained with me."

Soon after leaving Leroux where he was to winter, Mackenzie had "to land on a small island to stop the leakage of the canoe, occasioned by the shot of an arrow under the water mark by some Indian children." They cleared the traverse to Grant's Point in a single day with sail hoisted and a freshening westward wind.

It was now September and they had only to climb the current and rapids of the Slave River to be home. It was not easy going. There were cold showery rains, but they hurried on through them. The canoe was run into a stump and filled with water before they could get to land. Then it was damaged on the men's shoulders while being carried across a portage, and had to be gummed several times. Paddles had to be made to replace those broken pushing up the rapids.

There were early warnings of winter. Overhead, flocks of birds were winging southward. It snowed, and during the night of their penultimate camp it froze hard. By now their clothes were rotting on their bodies.

Saturday, Sept. 12.—The weather was cloudy, and also very cold. At night, we embarked with a North-East wind and entered the Lake of the Hills [the Athabasca]. About ten, the wind veered to the West-ward, and was as strong as we could bear it with the high sail, so that we arrived at Chepewyan fort by three o'clock in the afternoon, where we found Mr. Macleod, with five men busily employed in building a new house. Here, then, we concluded this voyage, which had occupied the considerable space of one hundred and two days.

The journey was a feat also of considerable determination and endurance. Mackenzie's tough French-Canadian voyageurs had borne him loyally and without complaint some three thousand miles over lake and stream, most of the distance upon Canada's longest river. The trip—which was started, remember, in the northern reaches of the Province of Alberta—was roughly equal to the distance by air from Quebec City to Vancouver. Remarkable though it was, however, the voyage was not much longer than the trip from Athabasca to Grand Portage and back, and perhaps not as difficult.

There must have been a considerable measure of disappointment in the failure to arrive at the Pacific after such an expense of time, toil and money. But Mackenzie's search was not over. There was perhaps another path from Chepewyan to the Pacific —up the Peace River.

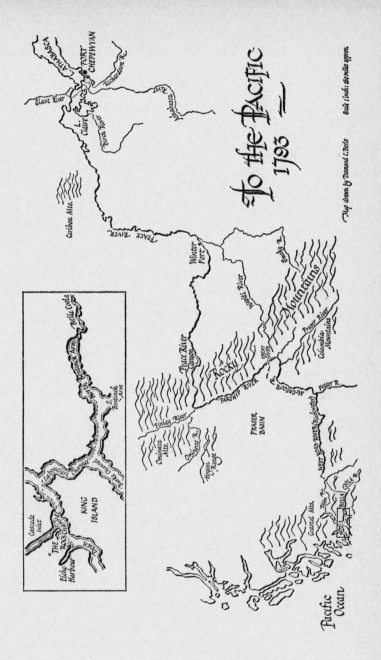

To the Pacific
1793

Map drawn by Desmond L. Berki

Scale 1 inch: 180 miles approx.

Chapter nine

Up the Peace

THE POSSIBILITY of reaching the Pacific by way of the Peace had been urged several years before. Alexander Henry had proposed the scheme to the Governor of Canada. He had even bragged that if he were a younger man without family responsibilities, he would tackle the job himself. Obviously the upstream Peace River road through the mountains was a more difficult journey than speeding west downstream from Slave Lake. Since no one really knew where either river highway led, Pond's more promising beliefs were easier to test first. Now that Mackenzie had proven them false, would the company risk another venture west?

After a winter's reflection on his travels, Mackenzie set out early in the summer of 1790 with the fur brigade for Grand Portage. The assembled partners listened to the report of his voyage and heard his suggestions for developing trade along the great river. He spoke of other plans for which it was vital that he be allowed a year's leave of absence from his department. The prize was a monopoly of trade along the West Coast. The matter was discussed, then a vote was taken.

They agreed he could go on furlough next summer. The partners were willing to support a second attack on the turreted mountain defences of the Pacific. And Mackenzie would lead it.

Back at Athabasca in the fall, he sent his cousin to build a post at the outlet of Great Slave Lake. Roderick was asked to find out all he could "about the large River which falls into the sea to the westward of the Grand River in which I voyaged."

In the spring Mackenzie left the Northwest for Montreal. Twelve years had gone by since he had begun his counting-house apprenticeship. Now he came back a man of some repute: a double shareholder in the North West Company, manager of the company's richest post, chief of the wintering bourgeois, and an accomplished traveller. Peter Pond was gone, having sold his share and retired to his birthplace; but surely Mackenzie paid a prideful visit to Mr. Gregory.

While it was still autumn, he boarded a sailing vessel for London. Mackenzie says that on his first journey, "I was not only without the necessary books and instruments, but also felt myself deficient in the science of astronomy and navigation." He wanted to get this knowledge before renewing his search for a practical trade route to the western shores of North America.

He didn't have much time for such study and learning. He shipped from England in April 1792, crossed the Atlantic, caught the Montreal freighters going to Grand Portage and there joined his department's canoes returning to Athabasca. Roderick, the silent partner of all his plans, had been advised to send men up the Peace beyond existing posts. They were to prepare materials for a new fort. "Whatever distance I could reach this fall would be an advancement of my voyage."

The brigade docked at Chepewyan on the tenth of October. Two days later Mackenzie entered the flat, alluvial mouth of the Peace. Six miles west of the junction of the Peace and Smoky rivers, not far from the present town of Peace River, "we landed on the first of November at my winter residence." They had arrived none too soon. At the end of October "the river began to run with ice, which we call the last of the navigation." He was a third of the way round the world from London and four hundred miles beyond Chepewyan; it was a good start for the next summer's journey.

Here the two men sent by Roderick had toiled since spring with axe, saw, plane and spade. They had cut over eight hundred logs, each eighteen feet long and seven inches in diameter— enough to make a palisaded wall 120 feet square. They had also dug a trench three feet deep in which to stand them. Piles of axe-squared timber and hand-sawn planks lay neatly stacked for the buildings. On the seventh, "I set all hands at work" to raise the walls and construct the proprietor's quarters and storehouses.

The place was well chosen. Westward was a ridge "inhabited by great numbers of deer." Across the river were "beautiful meadows with various animals grazing on them and groves of poplars irregularly scattered over them." They would live free from want.

Before November was out, winter clutched and clawed at the canvas camp. The unrelenting cold caught even the mighty motion of the river. From bank to bank its surface hardened and daily thickened. So severe was the frost on the twenty-seventh that the axes of the workmen shattered like glass. At that time Mackenzie and his men were still in tents. When he moved into his completed house two days before Christmas, the men began work on shelters for themselves.

On January 10 Mackenzie noted in his journal that "among the people here were two Rocky Mountain Indians. These men informed me that there is a great river whose current runs towards the mid-day sun and that the distance from it is not great across the mountains." That river, which he was sure emptied into the Pacific, was his goal.

In the early part of April, Mackenzie was busy trading with the Indians and preparing for his westerly trip. Six Canadians "who agreed to accompany me on my voyage of discovery" were engaged; so were a couple of Indian hunters. Old canoes were repaired; new ones were built. Cargoes of furs and pemmican were sent on the eighth of May to Fort Chepewyan, and Mackenzie "closed the business of the year for the company by writing my public and private despatches." He was ready to leave.

The canoe was put into the water. Her dimensions were twenty-five feet long within, exclusive of the curves of stem and stern, twenty-six inches hold, and four feet nine inches beam. At the same time she was so light that two men could carry her on a good road three or four miles without resting.

In this slender vessel, we shipped provisions, goods for

presents, arms, ammunition, and baggage to the weight of three thousands pounds, and an equipage of ten people: Alexander Mackay, Joseph Landry, Charles Ducette, François Beaulieux, Baptist Bisson, François Courtois, and Jacques Beauchamp, with two Indians as hunters and interpreters. [Landry and Ducette had been with him to the Arctic. There was also a dog.]

With these persons I embarked at seven in the evening. My people offered their prayers that we might return in safety.

A liquid avalanche rushed unceasingly at them, for the Peace was still in spring flood. The canoe was kept in the eddy currents near the shore; but where the river narrowed, it was too swift and strong for them to advance by paddle. So they had to push upstream, using poles ten feet long and tipped with iron. These were set on the river bottom close by the bank; then the men shoved, recovered, set the poles and thrust hard again. All day, sometimes, they travelled this way: flexing forearms, biceps and shoulders, moving the canoe roughly its own length every fifteen seconds—a speed of not much better than a mile an hour. It was sometimes faster and easier than hauling by line.

For ten days, from four in the morning to seven in the evening, the expedition struggled with pole and paddle against a rising current. Cliffs crowned with forests rose sheer out of the water; in other places, sloping gently away from the side of the river, were grassy plains and uplands teeming with "vast herds of elk and buffalo." They also saw dark, huge bears, "grisly and hideous," prowling the banks in search of prey. The weather was generally cold, often rainy, and on a couple of nights it froze hard. However progress was fairly steady at about fifteen miles a day—until Sunday May 19. Then the river stiffened its challenge.

On that day, "as the current threatened to be very strong, Mr. Mackay, the two hunters, and myself, went on shore in order to lighten the canoe." Following a beaten path, they climbed some cypress-covered hills "and before we had walked a mile, fell in with a herd of buffaloes with their young ones. We sent our dog after the herd, and a calf was soon secured by him. While the young men were skinning the animal, we heard two reports of fire arms from the canoe, which we answered as it was a signal for my return. We then heard another and immediately hurried down the hill."

At the river's edge, one of the Canadians told Mackenzie that the canoe was not far away "at the foot of a very strong rapid." He marched downstream, annoyed by the sharp summons of gunfire and by the men's indecision, for he had given instructions "that the river should be followed as long as it was practicable." Apparently the men, whose job was paddling rivers and portaging canoes, judged this bit of river "impracticable," hence the musket-shots.

There was a portage path where the men had halted. They had stopped there because they thought that this was the "day's march" around "a considerable succession of rapids, cascades, and falls" which the Rocky Mountain Indians "never attempted to ascend." But Mackenzie, who gave the orders, looked upstream. "By crossing to the other side, the river appeared to me passable." So, while Mackay and the young Indian hunters remained watching on the bank, Mackenzie made the traverse from west to east shore with his anxious voyageurs.

They reached an island and hauled alongside to its end, where the current threw the canoe "on a stony shore." Repairs were made, the baggage dried, vessel and stores carried across the end of the island. Then they worked upriver about three-quarters of a mile.

Ahead of them, in sudden white fury, the swift stream crashed into steep, overhanging rocky banks. Below, the water tumbled over rapids. Stretching across the river, like "so many large tables," were rocks with tops worn flat by centuries of rushing spring floods. "From one to the other of these islands," Mackenzie chanced a recrossing. Each minor traverse was alarmingly perilous, for the current raced with awesome force towards the lower cascades. "If we had got among them, it would have involved us and the canoe in common destruction."

They made it. Now the Canadians picked their way along a craggy bank, the canoe tugging at the end of the sixty-fathom line. Again Mackenzie, Mackay, and the hunters climbed upwards to walk high above the bent, straining voyageurs.

After striding several hours through spruce, birch and poplar forest, Mackenzie came to where the bank dropped low and where "the river flows in a channel of about one hundred yards broad" between the foot of a mountain and a high ridge. A short distance ahead "it rushes on between perpendicular rocks where it is not much more than half that breadth."

When the men arrived with the canoe, "we crossed over and camped on the opposite beach." The day's progress was seven miles; its labours and dangers were a muted introduction to things to come.

Hugging the river's edge, they entered the walled confines of the Peace River Canyon early next morning. Soon they came to the foot of an enormous rock. Mackenzie dared not skirt its base for fear that the current might sweep the canoe and its occupants downstream. He chose three men to go with him over the rock barrier.

It was fortunately soft "so that we were able to cut steps in it for twenty feet. At the hazard of my life I leaped on a small rock below where I received those who followed me on my shoulders." Now they pulled canoe, baggage and paddlers up and around to them.

With the iron-tipped poles they fought onward until the shore water deepened. Then they towed along a very steep bank, maintaining a precarious foothold by clinging to tree branches. Once when they stopped to rest someone forgot to fasten the towing-rope firmly to shore and the canoe sprang away with the current. A Canadian, so transfixed with tiredness and tension that he had not loosened his grip on the line, was able to hold the canoe until the others helped pull it back.

In the afternoon within a distance of two miles "we were obliged to unload four times and carry everything but the canoe." At five they reached a spot "where the river was one continued rapid." Again they picked up the tow-rope and stepped nervously upon shelving rocks.

At length the agitation of the water was so great that a wave striking on the bow of the canoe broke the line. It appeared impossible that the vessel could escape being dashed to pieces and those in her perishing. Another wave drove her out of the tumbling water so that the men were able to bring her ashore. Though she had been carried over rocks by these swells which left them naked a moment after, the canoe had received no injury.

In thirteen hours they had gone about five miles. The men were now so worn out and frightened that it would have been foolhardy to continue, for "the river above us, as far as one could see, was one white sheet of foaming water."

Some began to complain that it was madness to go on and that they ought to quit and go back. Mackenzie ordered camp made up on the bank and then set off with one of the Indians to examine the river while there was light. It was all rapids and cascades. "We returned from this reconnoitring excursion with our shoes worn out and wounded feet."

"It rained in the morning and did not cease till about eight. As the men had been very fatigued and disheartened, I permitted them to rest till that hour." Mackay, with three Canadians and the two Indian hunters, was sent "to keep the line of the river until they should find it navigable," and to scout a suitable portage path. Two were told to come back with information, "while the others were to go in search of the Indian carrying-place" whose entrance had been passed downstream. "The people who remained with me were employed in gumming the canoe and making handles for axes."

At sunset Mackay returned; the others came into camp two hours later. They had walked beyond the rapid to where the canoe could be safely launched. They had taken different routes back and both agreed that their outward course, about three leagues long, which "had penetrated thick woods, ascended hills and sunk into valleys," was the one to follow.

All went to rest, their courage and determination to push forward on the voyage renewed by a kettle of wild rice sweetened with sugar, and "their usual regale of rum."

At break of day the men began to cut a road up the mountain. As the trees were but of small growth, I ordered them to fell those which they found convenient, in such a manner that they might fall parallel with the road but, at the same time, not separate them entirely from the stumps so that they might form a kind of railing on either side.

The baggage was now brought from the water side to our camp. This was, from the steep shelving of the rocks, a very perilous undertaking as one false step of any of the people employed in it would have been instantly followed by falling headlong into the water. [Then it took the whole party to move the canoe up to the campsite.]

As soon as we had recovered, we advanced with the canoe up the mountain, having the line doubled and fastened successively to the stumps as we went on. A man at the end of the line hauled it around a tree, holding it on and shifting it as we proceeded. We got everything to the summit by two in the afternoon.

At five, armed with axes, the Canadians began to clear and widen "a well-beaten elk path." The trees were large, but there was little undergrowth. Before retiring they had advanced the portage about a mile, and at four the next morning they began to carry canoe and baggage.

Meanwhile, Mackenzie, Mackay and the hunters continued the labour of chopping a road two miles through "country overspread with the trunks of trees laid low by fire some years ago. Large copses, intermixed with briars, had sprung a close growth so as to render the passage through them painful and tedious." At four the carriers caught up with them and "at five, in a state of fatigue that may be more readily conceived than expressed, we camped near a rivulet or spring that issued from beneath a large mass of ice and snow."

Friday May 24 was the third and last trail-blazing day.

We continued our very laborious journey which led us down some steep hills and through a wood of tall pines. After much toil and trouble in bearing the canoe through the difficult passages which we encountered, at four in the afternoon we arrived at the river with all our baggage. I compute the distance of this day's progress to be about four miles.

About two hundred yards below us, the stream rushed with an astonishing but silent velocity between perpendicular rocks, not more than thirty-five yards asunder. When the water is high, it runs over those rocks in a channel three times that breadth and bounded by far more elevated precipices. In the former are deep round holes, some of which are full of water while others are empty, in whose bottom are small round stones as smooth as marble. Some of these natural cylinders would contain two hundred gallons.

Below the first of these rocks, the channel widens in a kind of zig-zag progression. It was really awful to behold with what infinite force the water drives against the rocks on one side and with what impetuous strength it is repelled to the other. It then falls back into a more straight but rugged passage, over which it is tossed in high, foaming, half-formed billows as far as the eye could follow.

After a night's rest, they made new setting poles and got ready to face the river again.

Chapter ten

Across the Great Divide

F OR A WEEK they poled, paddled, and carried through show-ers and chilling cold. At the end of May they saw "a chain of mountains running South and North as far as the eye could reach." Two or three miles further on "we arrived at the fork."

They had come to the junction of the Parsnip from the south and the Finlay from the north. A Rocky Mountain Indian who had visited Mackenzie's winter camp on the Peace River advised him to follow the south branch. That way, he said, "we should arrive at a carrying place to another river where the inhabitants build houses and live upon islands. I did not doubt that if I could get into the other river I should reach the ocean."

But the outward course had already drained reserves of strength and spirit, and still the river resisted relentlessly. "Indeed, the rush of water was so powerful that we were the greatest part of the afternoon in getting two or three miles." So, the attack on the forest-fringed Parsnip was begun in discontent and tiredness. Weary of the battle, they surrendered to fear and despair; so too, for a moment, did Mackenzie.

On the first of June, for example, "towards the dusky part of the evening, we heard several discharges from the fowling pieces of our people. We answered to inform them of our position." Mackay and the Indians, walking along the bank, had not been able to keep up with the canoe. They stumbled through the dark and came abreast of the evening camp. It was on an island. Into the river they plunged, swam across to their companions around the bright supper fire and arrived "in a state of fatigue and alarm."

One of the Indians was sure he had heard gunfire upriver as well as the camp's reply. Those at camp imagined they heard two more shots than the others actually made. Because they had seen along the Peace signs of the far-ranging, warlike Knisteneaux or Cree, the hunters suspected a war-party was near. "If they were numerous, we should have no reason to expect the least mercy from them in this distant country."

Mackenzie did not share in the panic. But "I thought it right, at all events, we should be prepared. Our fusees were therefore primed and loaded. Having extinguished our fire, each of us took his station at the foot of a tree where we passed an uneasy and restless night." Nothing happened. A clear pleasant morning dissolved the night's unsettling fears.

Three days later Mackenzie went on shore with the hunters and Mackay "to ascend an adjacent mountain with the hope of obtaining a view of the interior part of the country." The Canadians, alone in the canoe, were to continue upstream. The rendezvous signal was two shots.

At the top of the hill Mackenzie shinned up a tall tree and viewed only encircling miles of hills, forest and mountains. They marched down and ahead to the river, and fired off two shots. There was no reply.

Mackay built a fire and remained with one Indian. Mackenzie trekked forward with the other to a long, straight stretch of river. The canoe was not in sight. The signal was repeated without any answering shots. Branches were sent drifting downstream "as notice of our situation." Mackenzie searched upstream until midday before returning to Mackay who, in the meantime, had explored three or four miles down the river. The Canadians and the canoe had not shown up.

"The Indians, who are inclined to magnify evils of any and every kind, had at once sent the canoe and everyone on board it to the bottom. They were already settling a plan to return upon a raft, as well as calculating the number of nights that would be required to reach their home." Mackenzie began to blame himself for leaving the canoe and was so distressed that he agreed "to the scheme which my hunters had formed for our return."

At six-thirty Mackay and one Indian set out to go down the

river as far as possible before nightfall and to continue in the morning to the previous campsite. Mackenzie would venture further upriver. "If we both failed to meet the canoe, it was agreed that we should return to the place where we now separated." Mackay departed. "We were preparing to make a bed of the branches of trees when we heard a shot, and soon after another, which was the notice agreed upon if Mr. Mackay and the Indian should see the canoe. That fortunate circumstance was also confirmed by a return of the signal from the people."

"It was almost dark when we reached the canoe, barefooted, and drenched with rain." Mackenzie was obviously relieved and glad to be reunited with his people. "They informed me that the canoe had been broken and that they had this day experienced much greater toil and hardships than on any former occasion." He estimated their distance at eight miles and suspected they had "relaxed in their exertions."

Very likely, however, the men were telling the truth, for next day between four-thirty and noon, "the current was so strong that it was impossible to stem it with the paddles. The depth was too great to receive any assistance from the poles, and the bank of the river was so closely lined with willows and other trees that it was impossible to employ the line." They went four miles. "The whole of this distance we proceeded by hauling the canoe from branch to branch."

Daily they battled the current, and eight or twelve miles was a discouragingly short gain. But eventually they won their victory over the river and then they covered about seventeen miles between camps. The current had slackened. Everyone was on the lookout for the carrying place. They did not discover it.

Unless they met some local Indians, "all that remained for us to do was to push forwards till the river would be no longer navigable." Mackenzie considered pitching camp further upstream and searching overland for the portage. If that should fail, he intended to reverse his direction and go up the Finlay branch.

The canoe was put on the river at half-past five, Sunday June 9, after a stormy night, and steered through a heavy mist. About three o'clock and sixteen miles up the river they smelled fire and shortly heard a great confusion in the woods. "Before we were half over the river which is not more than a hundred yards wide, two men appeared on a rising ground over against us, brandishing their spears and displaying their bows and arrows." The interpreter explained that these were white people in the canoe who desired only to be friends. "They threatened if we came over before they were more fully satisfied of our peaceable intentions, that they would discharge their arrows at us."

After some time had passed hearing and answering their questions, they consented to our landing, though not without betraying fear and distrust. However, they laid aside their weapons. When I stepped forward and took each of them by the hand, one of them with a very tremulous action drew his knife from his sleeve, and presented it to me as a mark of his submission to my will and pleasure. They examined us and everything about us with a minute and suspicious attention. They had heard of white men, but this was the first time they had ever seen a human being of a complexion different from their own.

The canoe was unloaded, baggage was carried uphill, the tents were pitched. One of the natives was sent to recall his relatives; for good reasons the other was kept with the expedition. Assembled, the Indians formed a small, frightened group, legs and feet all scratched and bleeding from their hurried flight through the woods. They were given pemmican, and "consoled with beads and other trifles which seemed to please them."

"When I thought that they were sufficiently composed, I sent for the men to my tent. They said that they were not acquainted with any river to the Westward." However, they had ironwork which had passed to them through the hands of several tribes and was obtained from "the sea coast or, to use their expression, the Stinking Lake, where people like us come in vessels as big as islands."

This was a discouraging account "from a people who I had every reason to suppose were well acquainted" with the region. The Pacific appeared to be far away still, more than forty days according to these Indians. The existence of a river flowing south, described by the old Rocky Mountain Indian as being within reasonable reach, was denied.

It seemed to Mackenzie that he had come to a dead end in the mountains. He could not follow overland "that chain of connexion by which these people obtain their iron-work." The expedition could not possibly carry enough food, presents, and ammunition to make such a journey safe and successful. To go on up the Parsnip now appeared pointless. Yet to go back to their fort "after all our labour, sufferings, and dangers was an idea too painful to indulge."

He decided to postpone further inquiry until the morning, and set about to win friends. The children were given sugar; the men "regaled with such provisions as I had." But the morning's description of the country was no different.

One of the Parsnip Indians hung about the fire talking to Mackenzie's interpreters.

I understood enough of his language to know that he mentioned something about a great river, at the same time pointing significantly up that which was before us. On my inquiring of the interpreter I was informed that he knew of a large river that runs towards the mid-day sun. A branch flowed near the source of that which we were now navigating. There were only three small lakes and as many carrying-places leading to a small river which discharges itself into the great river. Its inhabitants built houses, lived on islands, and were numerous and warlike.

I desired him to describe the road with a piece of coal on a strip of bark—which he accomplished to my satisfaction. My hopes were now renewed. One of the Indians was persuaded by presents to accompany me as a guide to the inhabitants on the small lakes.

Mackenzie got the men smartly breaking camp and loading the canoe. While they were busy, he pencilled a description of the natives, their dress, weapons, utensils, and so on. The hunters bartered for "two quivers of excellent arrows, a collar of white bear's claws of great length, and horn bracelets. At ten, we were ready to embark."

Against a weak current they made good time now. The river, twisting in every direction, narrowed to fifteen yards. When they had gone about forty-five miles beyond the guide's camp, they left the main stream of the Parsnip. It was not more than ten yards wide.

The tributary which they followed was even narrower, with almost no current. There were so many sharp bends and turns in it that sometimes "we found it difficult to work the canoe forward." A mile up this slender channel was a lake, its entrance choked with driftwood fallen down from the mountain sides.

"The water however was so high that the country was entirely overflowed, and we passed with the canoe among the branches of trees. We advanced about a mile in the lake and took up our station for the night." It was Wednesday June 12 and they were on the headwaters of Peace River. The place has been fittingly named the Arctic Lake.

They broke camp between three and four in the morning, paddled to the end of the lake, landed and unloaded. "We found a beaten path leading over a low ridge of land eight hundred and seventeen paces in length." The portage ran between two mountains, rocky precipices on both sides. "Here two streams tumble down the rocks from the right and lose themselves in the lake which we had left. Two others fall from the opposite heights and glide into the lake which we were approaching." Its name is now Portage Lake.

From here on the waters ran to the Pacific. They had crossed the Great Divide.

Chapter eleven

Turnabout

THE EXPEDITION left Pacific Lake, the last of the three small lakes, and entered a tiny river with just enough water to float the canoe. Gradually it was deepened and widened by the waters of countless little streams rilling down the mountains. Banks of gravel, and fallen trees which had to be chopped clear, obstructed their way. "At half past six we were stopped by two large trees that lay across the river. It was with great difficulty that the canoe was prevented from driving against them. Here we unloaded and formed our encampment."

The guide pointed to a mountain beside the river that they were seeking and then asked if he could now go home. "He had been very much alarmed in going down some of the rapids with us." Maybe he knew what was in store.

Early next day "the men began to cut a road in order to carry the canoe and lading beyond the rapid. By seven they were ready." To lighten the canoe, Mackenzie planned to walk along the bank with Mackay and the Indians. But the Canadians "with great earnestness requested me to embark, declaring that if they perished I should perish with them."

We pushed off and proceeded but a very short way when the canoe struck. Notwithstanding all our exertions, the strength of the current was so great as to drive her sideways down the river and break her by the first bar. I instantly jumped into the water and the men followed my example. But before we could set her straight or stop her, she came to deeper water.

Like some crazy careening monster, the canoe wrenched out of control. All the men pulled themselves desperately over the gunwales, except one left thrashing and struggling against the current. The others had no time to grab paddles and check its runaway wildness.

We had hardly regained our places when we drove against a rock which shattered the stern of the canoe. It held only by the gunwales and the steersman could no longer keep his place. The force of this stroke drove us to the opposite side of the narrow river where the bow met with the same fate as the stern. At this moment the foreman seized on some branches of a small tree in the hope of stopping the canoe.

He did not succeed. The current propelled the canoe forward. As the foreman hung grimly on, the tree bent like a great bow. For a second or two he lay suspended over the river and then, as the branches snapped back, he was shot sprawling onto the bank.

"In a few moments we came across a cascade which broke several large holes in the bottom of the canoe and started all the bars except one behind the scooping seat." These flattening blows spread frame and bark over the water like a raft and so prevented the canoe from capsizing and dumping its occupants into the rapids. Mackenzie shouted to them to hold fast to the wreck.

We most fortunately arrived in shallow water and a small eddy where we were able to make a stand, more from the weight of the canoe resting on the stones than from any exertions of our exhausted strength. Though our efforts were short, they were pushed to the utmost as life or death depended on them.

This alarming scene with all its terrors and dangers occupied only a few minutes. We called to the people on shore to come to our assistance. The foreman had escaped unhurt from the extraordinary jerk with which he was thrown out of the boat. He appeared to give his assistance just as we were beginning to take our effects out of the water. The Indians, instead of making the least effort to help us, sat down and gave vent to their tears.

As the shock of the astonishing river ride wore off, some began to declare that it was now impossible to go on. "We were without a canoe and all the bullets were sunk in the river." Mackenzie waited "till their panic was dispelled." When "they had got themselves warm and comfortable with a hearty meal and rum enough to raise their spirits," he spoke to them.

"I brought to their recollection that I did not deceive them. Before they engaged to accompany me, they were made acquainted with the difficulties and dangers they must expect to encounter. I urged the honour of conquering disasters. Nor did I fail to mention the courage and resolution which was the peculiar boast of the North men. It would be a disgrace to give up and return home. Their own skills could repair the wreck of the canoe. Bullets could be made from the lead shot which they still had."

The work of repairing the canoe was started right away and Mackenzie himself joined in it. The day's escapes were not all over. Everything had been spread out to dry, including the gunpowder, eighty pounds of it. "One of the men carelessly walked across it with a lighted pipe in his mouth. One spark might have put a period to all my anxiety and ambition."

"With some pieces of oil cloth, plenty of gum, and a small roll of indifferent bark," the canoe was made serviceable again by the end of the following day. Two Canadians sent to survey the way ahead returned "with their clothes torn into tatters and their skin lacerated from passing through the woods." They brought back an account of a river so full of rapids and fallen trees that "we should have to carry the whole way."

It was an accurate forecast. From dawn to dusk for three days, they hacked at the forest to clear a trail "through low, swampy country." Across it, persecuted by swarms of mosquitoes and sand flies, they toted more than a thousand pounds of freight, usually in the heat of the day. Sometimes the canoe could be loaded to bear the cargo along a short stretch of river; more often the path had to be made wider so it could be carried too.

The canoe, patched with layers of additional gum and bark, was burdensome now. "Two men could not carry her more than a hundred yards without being relieved." Beneath its weight they staggered and swayed through deep mud, watchful for tree trunks and snaring roots. "One false step might have fateful consequences."

By noon on the third day they had gone less than ten miles. In what was left of a fourteen-hour workday they cut a three-quarter-mile path "through a continued swamp." Then they carried the canoe and a dozen ninety-pound packages to the bank of "the great river." In many places "we waded up to the middle of our thighs. It was eight in the evening when we arrived on the bank of a navigable river."

The "navigable river" was the McGregor, a major tributary of the Fraser. Reaching it was a triumph of strength and will. But Mackenzie had yet to learn that "the great river"—the Fraser—was not navigable for its whole length.

They camped, but without the guide, who escaped late one night. Next morning "before eight, we were on the water and driven by a strong current." For forty days they had crept painfully up the Peace and Parsnip rivers, carted over the Divide, and cut roads almost clear down "the bad river." But Tuesday June 18 was trouble-free and the canoe soared along the McGregor and the Fraser. They travelled fifty-five miles. One wonders if the Canadians sang.

The pace did not last. Morning mists, "so thick that we could not see the length of the canoe," screened approaches to rapids and cascades. Not till the fog lifted could they risk full-speed travel. Around the Red Rock or Fort George Canyon they took four hours widening a half-mile path and struggling with canoe and baggage "over a rocky and most rugged hill."

Indeed, their vessel had become "so weighted with extra gum and bark" that next day at Cottonwood Canyon "the men preferred running the rapid to carrying overland. Although they kept clear of the rocks, the water was so strong that the canoe filled as they drove down the rapid. Fortunately she did not overset. Having got her into an eddy, they emptied her and in a half-drowned condition arrived safe on shore."

In the early afternoon of their fourth day on the Fraser, they noticed a canoe on the edge of the woods, and then another being paddled by a lone Indian out of the mouth of a small side-stream.

He no sooner saw us than he gave the whoop to alarm his friends who immediately appeared on the bank armed with bows and arrows, and spears. They threatened us with instant death if we drew near the shore and followed the menace by discharging a volley of arrows. Some fell short of the canoe; others passed over it.

As the expedition retreated to the opposite bank, a canoe with two Indians in it set out downriver to sound a warning and to call up support. At any moment excited and hostile reinforcements might descend on them.

Leaving the canoe, Mackenzie walked along the beach by himself. He hoped that the Indians, seeing him alone, would respond to his signs of friendship; but he took no foolish chances. One of the hunters was directed "to slip into the woods with my gun and his own, and to conceal himself. He had orders to keep as near me as possible without being seen. If any of the natives should cross and attempt to shoot me from the water, it was his instructions to lay him low. He was particularly commanded not to fire till I had discharged one or both of the pistols that I carried in my belt. However if any of them were to land, he was to join me immediately."

The scheme worked:

Two of the natives came in a canoe but stopped when they had got within a hundred yards. I made signs for them to land and displayed looking-glasses, beads, and other alluring trinkets. At length they approached the shore, stern foremost, but would not land. I made them a present of some beads, with which they were going to push off.

I renewed my entreaties and after some time prevailed on

them to come ashore and sit down by me. My hunter now thought it right to join me, and created some alarm in my new acquaintances. It was soon removed and I had the satisfaction to find that he and these people perfectly understood each other. I instructed him to say everything that might tend to soothe their fears and win their confidence.

The Indians were too cautious and timorous to stay more than a little while. They returned to their waiting friends on the other side of the river where all could be seen examining the gifts and consulting for about fifteen minutes. Then Mackenzie and his followers were invited to join them. More presents were handed about and the children treated with sugar.

According to their account, this river runs towards the midday sun. At its mouth white people were building houses. They represented its current to be strong. In three places it was altogether impassable from the falls and rapids which poured along between perpendicular rocks much higher, and more rugged, than any we had yet seen, and that would not admit of any passage over them. The inhabitants were numerous; their immediate neighbours, a very malignant race.

When the Indians learned that Mackenzie intended to go on to the Pacific, they advised against it "as we should certainly become a sacrifice to the savage spirit of the natives." Just then a small canoe was seen, coming in answer to the summons for help. There were three men in it. One of them "advised us to delay our departure for that night. Their relations, having by now been alarmed by the messengers, would certainly oppose our passage even if I had two of their own people with me."

So, "I passed the rest of the day with these people. They consisted of seven families containing eighteen men; they were clad in leather, and handsome beaver and rabbitskin blankets. They had not been long in this country where they proposed to catch fish for their winter provisions."

At six next morning, Saturday June 22, the small canoe carrying two Indians and Mackay went ahead. The expedition's canoe, in which the third native sat with Mackenzie, followed. Twelve miles downstream they stopped for half an hour at another summer fishing camp. Its inhabitants at first were threatening, but the guides' explanations and a few presents relaxed their fears. However, "I gave them a specimen of the use to which we applied our firearms. At the same time I calmed their astonishment by the assurance that though we could at once destroy those who did us injury, we could equally protect those who shewed us kindness. We left these people with favourable impressions of us."

Three miles on they landed at another camp. The appearance of the natives here "was more wild and ferocious than any whom we had yet seen. Indeed I was afraid that our guides would fall prey to their savage fury." But they too were calmed. Mackenzie then shook hands all round with sixteen men and several women, though this form of greeting had to be explained as the white man's peculiar token of friendship.

Attracted by the man's face, Mackenzie asked an elderly Indian "to draw a sketch of the country upon a large piece of bark. He immediately entered on the work, frequently appealing to and sometimes asking the advice of those around him."

He described the river as running to the East of South and every six or eight leagues encumbered with falls and rapids, some of which were very dangerous, and six of them impracticable. The carrying-places he represented as of great length, and passing over hills and mountains. He depicted the lands of three other tribes, in succession, who spoke different languages. Beyond them he knew nothing either of the river or country, only that it was still a long way to the sea.

His people had in former years obtained small amounts of metal and trinkets by trading down the Fraser. But now they travelled westward over an easily followed trail for these articles. It took them six nights. They carried "dressed leather, and beaver, bear, lynx, fox and marten skins" to exchange for copper and brass, out of which they made "collars, arm-bands, bracelets, and other ornaments," and for bar iron, eighteen by two inches, which they shaped into axes and, when these wore out, into arrowheads and spearheads. The Indians with whom they traded had told them that three days' journey away the white men were building houses.

Given this crude sketch of the peoples and geography of the region, Mackenzie had some hard thinking to do—and a crucial decision to make.

There were strong reasons against continuing down the river. His men thought "that it would be absolute madness to attempt a passage through so many savage and barbarous nations." Supplies were low; they had but a month's provision, only 150 bullets, thirty pounds of shot, and too few goods with which to purchase goodwill and assistance from the residents of the river. Finally, the Fraser was reportedly long and dangerous to descend. It would likely be so laborious and time-consuming to return that "I must give up returning this season to Athabasca."

There was a single argument for advance: turning back "could not fail to cool the ardour, slacken the zeal, and weaken the confidence of those who have no greater inducement to the undertaking than to follow the conductor of it."

In the morning Mackenzie called the Indians together in the hope of getting more information. The descriptions of the previous day were repeated, but he also learned that on their overland trade trips they left the Fraser by way of a small river flowing from the west, paddled four days and walked two days. Mackenzie was told that he would have to leave his larger craft behind, but that the Indians with whom they traded had "wooden canoes much larger than ours, in which they go down a river to the sea." The distance "to the lake whose water is nauseous" was a day's travel.

It was now absolutely necessary that I should come to a final determination which route to take. No long interval of reflection was employed before I preferred to go over land. The comparative shortness and security of such a journey were alone sufficient to determine me. I accordingly proposed to two of the Indians to accompany me, and one of them readily assented.

Mackenzie now convened his crew and went over the arguments which led him to prefer trying the westward road to the sea. However, he said that he would not attempt the overland route unless they would agree to return—if that way should prove impassable—and "continue our voyage to the discharge of the waters, whatever the distance might be." Mackenzie's decision to postpone the flight down the Fraser and to walk over a mountain trade trail was happily received by those who did the journey's hard work.

Orders were issued for an immediate departure. The guide was notified. Some presents were distributed. An Indian woman who had been given a mooseskin to make some shoes was rewarded with a few beads, "considered a sufficient remuneration for the skill employed on them."

"Mr. Mackay, by my desire, engraved my name, and date of the year on a tree."

On Sunday June 23 the expedition checked its descent of the Fraser, turned about, and headed north for a footpath leading west across the mountains to the sea. That journey was to prove neither so short nor so safe as Mackenzie's reflections had supposed.

Chapter twelve

Alarm on the Fraser

THE NEXT TEN DAYS, through the close of June and the beginning of July, have a queer, disturbed quality of nightmarish confusion and uncertainty. The purpose and will of the trip faltered temporarily. For a while, Mackenzie lost control of affairs.

When the expedition was packed and ready to leave, the guide declared a preference to go overland to his lodge. Well aware now of the unreliability of guides, Mackenzie would rather have had him in the canoe; but he could hardly refuse. Mackay and the two hunters were assigned to join the young man.

The canoe was paddled away at ten in the morning, and the two groups met a few miles upstream at a prearranged rendezvous. The guide still wished to continue along the bank, so Mackay and the hunters remained with him. The canoe, patched, cumbersome, and out of trim, was driven forward at a surprisingly good clip, but not fast enough to reach their campsite of June 21-22.

After sharing an encampment with a couple of families seen two days earlier, the expedition departed at four in the morning. At eight they arrived at the place where they had first contacted the Indians. Mackay and the two hunters were already here—looking very scared. The guide had vanished; the lodges were empty. Something had gone wrong.

Mackay had a strange story to tell. Soon after he had parted from Mackenzie for the second time, "they met a party of Indians whom we had known at this place and who appeared in a state of extreme rage, their bows bent and arrows across them. The guide stopped to ask them some questions which my people did not understand, and then set off with his utmost speed." Mackay managed to keep pace—a tribute to his fitness—until both were worn out with running. All the guide would say was that the Indians they had met "were going to do mischief, but refused to name the enemy."

The guide then raced off again, Mackay and the hunters hanging on as well as they could. At ten in the evening, the crazy cross-country chase was still in progress. Eventually "they all laid down, exhausted with fatigue, and without any kind of covering. They were cold, wet, and hungry, but dared not light a fire for fear of some enemy."

This comfortless spot they left at dawn and on their arrival at the lodges found them deserted, the property of the Indians scattered about as if abandoned for ever. The guide then made two or three trips into the woods, calling aloud and bellowing like a madman. At length he set off in the same direction as they had come, and had not since appeared.

To heighten their misery, as they did not find us at the place appointed, they concluded that we were all destroyed. They had already formed their plan to take to the woods and cross in as direct a line as they could to the waters of the Peace River. They intended to have waited for us till noon, and if we did not appear by that time, to have entered without further delay on their desperate expedition.

The canoe had arrived with four hours to spare.

The relating of this lunatic episode threw the men into a panic. However, Mackenzie ordered the canoe unloaded except for some lading as ballast, left four men at the spot, and returned to the last night's camp. "I hoped to find the two men, with their families, whom we had seen there, and to bring them to camp with us, when I should wait the issue of this mysterious business." When he got there, he found that they "had quitted their sheds in the silence of the night, and had not taken a single article of their property with them." He returned to the others.

78

For the physical safety of himself and his followers, Mackenzie said that he had no fear "even if their whole force should have been combined to attack us." What really worried him was the loss of the guide and the unsuccessful continuation of the journey. To the frightened requests of his crew to embark and withdraw from the danger zone, he paid no attention. The canoe was ordered out of the river. "To add to our distress we had not an ounce of gum, and not one of the men had sufficient courage to venture into the woods to collect it."

"We now took a position that was best calculated for defence, got our arms in complete order, filled each man's flask of powder, and distributed a hundred bullets, which were all that remained, while some were employed in melting down shot to make more." During these preparations, an Indian came down the river in a canoe, landed, examined the empty lodges, refused to be friendly, and "even threatened that he would hasten to join his friends, who would come and kill us."

As a precaution, Mackenzie shifted the campsite to the very edge of the river.

I ordered the canoe to be loaded, and dropped to an old house, one side of which, with its roof, had been carried away by the water. But the three remaining walls were sufficient to shelter us from the woods. I then ordered two strong piquets to be driven into the ground, to which the canoe was fastened. If we were hard pressed we had only to step on board and push off.

We were under the necessity of making a smoke to keep off the swarms of flies which would have otherwise tormented us; but we did not venture to let it blaze as it would have been a mark for the arrows of the enemy. Mr. Mackay and myself, with three men, kept alternate watch, and allowed the Indians to do as they fancied. I took the first watch and the others laid down in their clothes by us. I also placed a sentinel at a small distance, who was relieved every hour. The weather was cloudy, with showers of rain.

At daylight the camp was moved back up to the Indian lodges. "Mr. Mackay informed me that the men had expressed their dissatisfaction to him in a very unreserved manner, and had in very strong terms declared their resolution to follow me no further in my proposed enterprise." Mackenzie pretended to take no notice. His mind was fixed on regaining the confidence of the natives and hiring a guide, "without whose assistance it would be impossible for me to proceed."

At twelve, while Mackenzie was busy observing the sun's meridian altitude and calculating latitude, an Indian drifting downstream on a raft noticed them, worked "very hard to get to the opposite shore where he soon landed, and instantly fled into the woods." Meanwhile "the men loaded the canoe without having received any orders from me. As this was the first time they had ventured to act in such a decided manner, I naturally concluded that they had a plan for their return."

Fear and discontent seemed to be approaching near mutiny. Mackenzie said nothing. He simply waited and watched. Then there was a distraction. "Our Indians perceived a person in the edge of the woods above us, and they were immediately dispatched to discover who it was. After a short absence they returned with a young woman whom we had seen before."

Her language was not understood by the interpreters so there was still no clue to the cause of the strange alarm among the natives. Apparently the woman had returned to fetch some things. She was treated kindly, given presents, and allowed to go.

At eight in the evening I ordered four men to step into the canoe and drop down to our guard-house. My command was instantly obeyed. The rest of us proceeded by land. When I was yet at a considerable distance from the house, having a bow and quiver in my hand, I thoughtlessly let fly an arrow. I heard it strike a log of the house. The men, who had just landed, imagined that they were attacked by an enemy from the woods. On my arrival I found that the arrow had passed within a foot of one of the men. Though it had no point, the weapon, incredible as it may appear, had entered a hard, dry log of wood upwards of an inch.

The offensive power of such weapons in the hands of the natives only excited the jumpy uneasiness of the men.

Mr. Mackay having the first watch, I laid myself down in my cloak. At midnight a rustling noise was heard in the woods. At one I took my turn of the watch, and our dog continued to run backwards and forwards along the skirts of the wood. At two in the morning the sentinel informed me that he saw something like a human figure creeping along on all-fours about fifty paces above us. His information was true. But when day appeared, it proved to be an old, grey-haired, blind man.

Too feeble to run away with the others, he had hidden in the woods until hunger drove him out. Directed to the fire and given food, he then explained "that very soon after we had left them, some natives arrived from above, who informed them that we were enemies. Our unexpected return, in direct contradiction to our own declarations, confirmed them in that opinion."

The old man told Mackenzie "that some of the natives whom I had seen here were gone up the river, and also that he expected a considerable number of his tribe to come on the upper part of the river to catch fish for their present support and to cure them for the winter. Among them he had a son and two brothers."

At last Mackenzie acted. "I informed the old man that he must accompany me. If we met with his son or brothers, I depended upon him to persuade them, or some of their party, to attend us as guides" overland. The old man was unwilling to leave, but Mackenzie ordered him carried to the canoe. "At seven in the morning we left this place, which I named Deserter's River or Creek." A creek, so named, is mapped flowing into the Narcosli Creek on the west side of the Fraser below Quesnel.

Our canoe was become so leaky, that it was absolutely unfit for service; and it was the unremitting employment of one person to keep her clear of water. We therefore inquired of the old man where we could obtain the articles necessary to build a new one, and we understood that some distance up the river we should find plenty of bark and cedar.

A small canoe with two Indians in it heading downstream skimmed past them without replying to any of the blind man's questions. At three in the afternoon they came to the mouth of the Quesnel River where the lodges were deserted. "About sunset the canoe struck upon the stump of a tree, which broke a large hole in her bottom," so they camped nearby.

The weather was fine when they paddled away from the evening campsite. Stops were made at eight and at noon to gather bark. "It now remained for us to fix on a proper place for building another canoe as our old one had become an absolute wreck. At five in the afternoon we came to a small island not much encumbered with wood. We landed." They camped here four days.

"At a very early hour of the morning, every man was employed in making preparations for building a canoe, and different parties went in search of wood, watape, and gum. At two in the afternoon they all returned successful, except the collectors of gum, and it was feared we should not obtain a sufficient supply of it. After a necessary refreshment, each began his respective work." They were bothered by hordes of insects, "particularly the sand fly, which I consider the most tormenting insect of its size in nature."

Provisions were running low:

I was compelled to put the people on short allowance and confine them to two meals a day, a regulation peculiarly offensive to a Canadian voyager. One of these meals was composed of the dried roes of fish, pounded, boiled in water, thickened with a small quantity of flour, and fattened with a bit of grain. These articles, brought to the consistency of a pudding, produced a substantial and not unpleasant dish. The natives are very careful of the roes of fish, which they dry and preserve in baskets made of bark. Those we used were found in the huts of the first people who fled from us.

Next day, with continuing fine weather, "at five o'clock we renewed our labour and the canoe was got in a state of considerable forwardness." Yet, Mackenzie decided to pep up the work, to stiffen the softening spine of the expedition, and to make it clear that his determination to reach the Pacific was still strong. He picked on the man in charge of canoe construction and began to scold. The work was going too slowly; they were eating instead of labouring; time was precious, food was short. He knew how scared they were and how eager to return to the Peace River, but whatever talks and plans they had about quitting the journey, he was still resolved to reach the ocean—no matter what dangers and difficulties should threaten them.

"The man was very much mortified at my addressing this remonstrance particularly to him, and replied that he did not deserve my displeasure more than the rest of them." The rest presumably were standing round and listening. "My object being answered, the conversation dropped and the work went on."

In the early afternoon a canoe paddled by two Indians appeared at the narrow, shallow thoroughfare between the island and the west bank. It halted, and turned back. Then, unlike those of the last few days, it appeared again and landed on the outside of the island.

The guide stepped out, full of apologies for abandoning them. "He assured me that since he had left me, his whole time had been employed in searching after his family who had been seized with the general panic, started by the false reports of the people who had first fled from us. The blind old man gave a very favourable account of us to his friends, and all three were very merry together during the whole of the afternoon."

The guide remained the following day and said that their friends were at the carrying-place around the rapids. When Mackenzie retired to his tent on this last day of June, he sat quietly in the dark watching because he had learned from one of his hunters that the old man intended to escape. "About twelve I observed the old man creeping on his hands and knees towards the waterside. We followed him very quietly to the canoe. He would have gone away with it if he had not been interrupted." Brought before his friends, he was rebuked by the guide, who "asked him how he could expect that the white people would return to this country if they experienced such ungrateful treatment."

Mackay was then wakened to watch while Mackenzie slept. When he rose, the guide was gone. From the interpreter he found out "that the guide had expressed his desire, as soon as the sun was up, to go where he might find his friends and there wait for us. I hoped that might be true."

At five in the afternoon our vessel was completed and ready for service. She proved a stronger and better boat than the old one, though had it not been for the gum obtained from the latter, it would have been difficult to have prevented her from leaking. The remainder of the day was employed by the people in cleaning and refreshing themselves, as they had enjoyed no relaxation from their labours since we had landed on this spot. We put our arms in order. They were at all times a general object of attention.

The canoe was loaded for departure by half past three on the morning of July 2. The blind Indian was offered a passage to his friends up the river. He preferred to stay on the island, so a few pounds of pemmican were given to him. The men had a dram of rum each, "a very comfortable treat," and then set to in high spirits. The island, now off their stern, Mackenzie named Canoe Island.

At eleven we arrived at the rapid. The foreman, who had not forgotten the fright he suffered on coming down it, proposed that the canoe and lading should be carried over the mountain. I threatened him with taking the office of foreman myself. As the water did not seem so strong on the West side, I first put Mr. Mackay and our two hunters on shore to try the woods for game.

The river was crossed and by shoving with the paddles they worked a considerable distance up alongside the rocks until they could go no further without the help of the towing-line. For three hundred feet ahead a giant rock rose high and straight out of the water. They could not paddle or pole against the current; they could not get any hold on the river-level edge of the rock face. The men suggested a return and a portage on the east side.

Mackenzie proposed a startling alternative. Two men were to take the sixty-fathom line, climb up the rock wall, cross the top, descend the other side, attach the end of the line to a roll of bark, and float it down to the waiting canoe. Then on a signal they were to haul. Four paddling and two pulling on the line would get them past the barrier.

In order to get to the water's edge on the other side of the rock, the men had to hitch one end of the line around a tree at the top and let themselves down. Mackenzie's idea worked. This technique was used once more, and twice the canoe was unloaded and carried around cascades. "We were not more than two hours getting up this difficult part of the river, including the time employed in repairing a hole which had been broken in the canoe by the negligence of the steersman."

There was evidence that the guide had passed the carrying-place, but there were no Indian camps. At ten the next morning "we came to a small river, which answered to the description of that whose course the natives said they follow in their journeys towards the sea coast. We therefore put into it and endeavoured to discover if our guide had landed here, but there were no traces of him or any others."

The nagging uncertainty, briefly dispelled by the reappearance of the guide at Canoe Island, was back one more. Mackenzie wasn't sure what to do. Heading upriver could mean possibly missing the natives and he thought his men would not want to return from an upstream camp. "As for attempting the woods without a guide to introduce us to the first inhabitants, that would be little short of madness." Mackenzie decided to share these problems with his troops, "and I experienced a considerable relief from this resolution."

They had suggestions. Some were for striking westward into the woods straight away; others proposed searching upriver for the guide or finding another one among the Indians. This is what Mackenzie decided to do. But first the woods around the West-Road River, which is what he named the place and what it is still called, were scouted in different directions. "I went some distance up the river myself, which I found to be navigable only for small canoes. Two of the men found a good beaten path, leading up a hill just behind us, which I imagined to be the great road."

Mackenzie also found out that the men had not come to any fixed determination among themselves to head home for the Peace River. The tension of the last few days had affected him too. He had imagined distrust and conspiracy where there had only been fright. Anyway, a feeling of team spirit and happy co-operation was regenerated and memories of the reproaches on Canoe Island were wiped away. At the same time their luck turned for the better.

At four in the afternoon they left the West-Road–Fraser Junction and headed up the latter river.

We had not been upon the water more than three-quarters of an hour when we saw two canoes coming with the stream. No sooner did the people in them perceive us than they landed, and we went on shore at the same place with them. They proved to be our guide, and six of his relations. He was covered with a painted beaver robe, so that we scarcely knew him in his fine clothes. He instantly desired us to acknowledge that he had not disappointed us, and declared at the same time that it was his constant intention to keep his word. I accordingly gave him a jacket, a pair of trowsers, and a handkerchief as a reward for his honourable conduct.

Next morning Mackay set off up the river with the Indian canoes, while Mackenzie stayed behind to cache those things that they could not take with them on the overland trails.

At our first hiding-place we left a bag of pemmican, weighing ninety pounds, two bags of wild rice, and a gallon keg of gunpowder. Before putting these articles in the ground, we rolled them up in oil cloth, and dressed leather. In the second hiding-place, and guarded with the same rollers, we hid two bags of Indian corn, or maize, and a bale of different articles of merchandize.

When we had completed this important object, we proceeded till half past eight and landed at the entrance of a small rivulet where our friends were waiting for us. Here it was necessary that we should leave our canoe and whatever we could not carry on our backs. First, we prepared a stage on which the canoe was placed bottom upwards, and shaded by a covering of small trees and branches to keep her from the sun. We then built an oblong hollow square, ten feet by five, of green logs, wherein we placed every article it was necessary for us to leave here, and covered the whole with large pieces of timber.

While we were employed in this business, our guide and his companions were so impatient to be gone that we could not persuade him to wait. [He left, but one of his friends stayed behind to show them the way.] . . . At noon we were ready to enter the woods.

The date was July 4. Now they began a long walk.

Chapter thirteen

Pacific pilgrimage

THEY TRUDGED through the woods, heavy bags on their backs. "Each of the Canadians had a burden of about ninety pounds, with a gun, and some ammunition. The Indians had about forty-five pounds weight of pemmican to carry, besides their guns, &c., with which they were very dissatisfied. My own load, and that of Mr. Mackay, consisted of twenty-two pounds of pemmican, some rice, a little sugar, &c., amounting in the whole to about seventy pounds each, besides our arms and ammunition. I also had the tube of my telescope swung across my shoulder which was a troublesome addition to my burthen." The food ration was two meals a day.

They climbed a hill for about a mile and a well-worn path took them over and through rugged forested country. At six-thirty they came to an Indian camp where the guide was waiting by one of its fires. They stayed the night here. As they lay down on the ground to sleep, bodies limp and aching from the new exercise, the Indians started to sing, softly and plaintively, without drumming, or rattling, or dancing. "It had somewhat the air of church music," and was a caressing, soothing end to the day.

A party of four Indians, lately back from a western barter trip, had shown up at sunset. In conversation around the evening fires, they described the road to the sea as an eight days' march and offered to send two young men with Mackenzie "to notify the different tribes that we were approaching so that they might not be surprised at our appearance, and be disposed to afford us a friendly reception." It was a welcome proposal.

For seven or eight days, Mackenzie was better served by guides than he had ever been. Except for two sections of the march, he was led along a trail, clearly marked from much use, that paralleled the West-Road River to its very source. The guides were willing, the interior mountain Indians generally friendly, and he was handed from group to group, the conductors often arranging their own substitutes. To warn camps of Indian families, the unburdened guides sometimes sped ahead faster than anyone could match, and usually they were found up the path, waiting for the plodding party.

There were some curious incidents on the way. While waiting for shoes to be made for a couple of guides at their first interior camp, Mackenzie bartered for two halfpence which hung as ornaments in some children's ears; one was English and "the other of the State of Massachussets, coined in 1787." New England Yankee ships were already rounding Cape Horn and trading along the northern Pacific coast.

Storm-showers and the soaking wet of all-night rains, like the loads on their backs, were among the constant hardships of the journey. For the first week it rained some part of every day; once the ground was strewn for two miles with hailstones. A drenching downpour in daytime would force them to stop and build a camp shelter, usually a hastily constructed shed of oil-cloth, and an overnight deluge would hold them up until the weather cleared, a fire could be lit, and their clothes stripped off and dried.

They ran short of food. The supplies they carried could be eaten without cooking, and these they were compelled to rely on. They were fortunate if they obtained half a dozen small dried or boiled fish from Indian encampments along the way. In twelve days the hunters' guns added only six birds to their scanty stores; two were eagles and three, grey partridges. "Foreseeing the difficulty of procuring provisions for our return," on July 9 and again on July 16 Mackenzie ordered a twenty-pound bag of pemmican buried under the campfire because "we found the country so destitute of game."

Rations had to be cut. Worried "that the distance from the sea might be greater than I had imagined, it became a matter of real necessity to diminish the consumption of our provisions and to subsist upon two-thirds of our allowance; a proposition as unwelcome to my people as it was necessary to put into immediate practice."

Wet, hungry, fly-bitten, they trod their winding Pacific pilgrimage: through pathless woods which slapped and dampened them with secret reserves of rain-drippings; around lakes and their bordering knee-deep swamps; along hard-packed trails topping steep valleys; across rising ground dense with trees; on open, level country; past dry or water-filled basins lined with gravel, or with grass, mustard and mint; across creeks, streams, and rivers, deep and narrow or wide and shallow, by wading, swimming, or rafting, or even by walking atop a beaver dam; beneath beautifully green hills or beside fire-wasted slopes; under and over the snagging, scratching branches of fallen timber to where the land was folded in ridges, barren and stony, with a few scattered cypress trees, and where the snowy peaks of the coastal range rose before them.

It was the anniversary of Mackenzie's arrival at the Arctic four years ago. They were near the upper waters of the West-Road River with a pair of reluctant, complaining guides. They had been engaged on July 10 from a lakeside lodge where some of the inhabitants "said it was a journey of four days to the sea, and others were of opinion that it was six; and there were among them those who extended it to eight." On the eleventh the guides declared their intention of leaving the expedition, and on the afternoon of the twelfth Mackenzie "was obliged to give them several articles, and promise more, in order to induce them to continue till we could procure other natives to succeed them."

At four o'clock on the same day, after fording a river, the guides set off so fast that Mackenzie could not follow. One of the hunters who did manage to catch up to them was told that they were going ahead "to prevent the people whom they expected to find from shooting their arrows at us." The expedition camped at seven without ever seeing the guides again.

They were stranded about half-way between the Fraser and

the coast. Not far from their stopping-place, a member of the expedition discovered a cross-road while he was gathering wood for the fire. Which was the Pacific road? The men were nervous.

Next day, the weather clear and cold, "about five, after we had warmed ourselves at a large fire, we proceeded on our dubious journey." An hour later they saw smoke coming from a house by the side of a small river. Followed most unwillingly by his party, Mackenzie hurried forward and was almost at the house when looking back, he suddenly realized he was fifty yards into an Indian defile, a long, narrowing, walled corridor designed to force any attackers to approach practically in single file.

Trapped in this nakedly dangerous position, Mackenzie was spotted. Suddenly women and children were screaming. He rushed into the house as a man escaped out the back door, but he imprisoned three women and their seven children. It was some time before they were quieted down and Mackenzie learned how lucky he had been. Most of the men were absent on a trading journey. Eventually an elderly man and his two sons were persuaded to return to the cabin. A number of presents were given out, and father and sons agreed to act as guides.

Their new guides struck out along a lake, through a swamp, and then climbed up a hill from whose summit "we had an extensive view to the South-East, from which direction a considerable river appeared to flow"—perhaps the Dean, which empties into the Pacific. That evening, after crossing the river on rafts, they camped. In the morning the old fellow went forward by himself, heading southwards towards the Bella Coola River. At eleven they caught up with him in the company of five men and their families.

Every man, woman, and child carried a burden, consisting of beaver coating and parchment, as well as skins of the otter, the marten, the bear, the lynx, and dressed moose-skins. The last they procure from the Rocky Mountain Indians. According to their account, the people of the sea coast prefer them to any other article. Several of their relations and friends, they said, were already gone, as well provided as themselves to barter with the people of the coast; who barter in their turn with white people who arrive there in large canoes.

Of few groups of Indians does Mackenzie speak so well as these. They were attractive, neat, clean, genuinely friendly, and seemed pleased to have Mackenzie's expedition attached to theirs. But by the next afternoon they had changed their mind and route; and in spite of Mackenzie's entreaties, they would not gratify his wish "to continue with them whatever way they went." But they sent for guides from a nearby tribe, and waited till they arrived, four of them.

While they waited, one of the Indians, because Mackenzie had mentioned the meagerness of the expedition's food supply, boiled up a kettle of fish-roes.

He took the roes out of a bag, and having bruised them between two stones, put them in water to soak. His wife then took a handful of dry grass in her hand, with which she squeezed them through her fingers. In the meantime her husband was gathering wood to make a fire for heating stones. When she had finished her operation, she filled a water kettle nearly full of water and poured the roes into it.

When the stones were sufficiently heated, some of them were put into the kettle and others were thrown in from time to time till the water was boiling. The woman also continued stirring the contents of the kettle till they were brought to a thick consistency. The stones were then taken out, and the whole was seasoned with about a pint of strong rancid oil. The smell of this curious dish was sufficient to sicken me without tasting it, but the hunger of my people surmounted the nauseous meal.

The old man had also remained until now and when the new guides arrived and proposed a route to the sea by way of their houses, he advised Mackenzie to continue "along the road which had already been marked out to us." The guides were agreeable and "pointed out to me the pass in the mountain, bearing South by East by compass." Ahead of them was the Rainbow Range.

Briefly met, all the interior travellers parted at four in the afternoon and went their different ways, Mackenzie and his new guides towards the south. In the closing hours of the day they began to climb and camped at nine "surrounded by mountains covered with snow"—and mosquitoes.

Before the sun rose in the morning, they went down into a lovely valley, fed on ground-hogs and claytonia root—"like a bunch of white berries of the size of a pea; its shape was that of a fig, while it had the colour and taste of a potato"—and started up the mountain pointed out the day before. They reached the compact snows of the pass, and soon after the Indians and hunters began to follow "the tracks of a herd of small deer which must have passed a short time before us."

Now a tempest of hail, snow and rain blew up. An hour and a half went by before the hunters returned with a small doe. "I proposed to leave half of the venison in the snow, but the men preferred carrying it, though their strength was very much exhausted."

They were in the southern extremity of what is now Tweedsmuir Provincial Park, and in a short while a glorious view opened in front of them. "Before us appeared a stupendous mountain whose snow-clad summit was lost in the clouds. Between it and our immediate course flowed the river to which we were going." The river, about twelve miles away, was the Bella Coola, and the mountain was likely the one now named Stupendous Mountain, mapped 8,500 feet high.

Though they were without rum, since all the casks had been left by the Fraser River, this was a time for celebration. "As soon as we could gather a sufficient quantity of wood, we stopped to dress some of our venison, and we made a heartier meal than we had done for many a day before. To this comfort I added that of taking off my beard, as well as changing my linen, and my people followed the humanising example." Not much of a ceremony maybe, but it was a ritual suited to the end of the trail, and a decent preparation before introducing themselves to a new people.

Their path was downwards. "We came to the brink of a precipice from whence our guides discovered the river to us and a village on its banks." Two hours saw them at the foot of the cliff, following a rocky creek bed, its spring flood line twelve feet higher than the present water level. "Here were also the loftiest elder and cedar trees that I had ever seen. We were now sensible of an entire change in the climate, and the berries were quite ripe." Near sunset, the guides forged in advance, leaving a trail of broken branches. Then the night closed round the expedition, and the men, tired and distrustful of the dark, wanted to camp.

But Mackenzie was exultant. He felt his way through the blackness to the edge of the woods, and then groped further on, followed with a pleading, warning hesitancy by his men, "till I arrived at a house, and soon discovered several fires in small huts, with people busily employed in cooking their fish."

I walked into one of them without the least ceremony, threw down my burden and, after shaking hands with some of the people, sat down upon it. They received me without the least appearance of surprise, but soon made signs for me to go up to the large house which was erected on upright posts at some distance from the ground. A broad piece of timber with steps cut in it led to the scaffolding even with the floor, and by this curious kind of ladder I entered the house at one end.

Having passed three fires at equal distances in the middle of the building, I was received by several people sitting upon a very wide board at the upper end of the room. I shook hands with them and seated myself beside a man, the dignity of whose countenance induced me to give him that preference. I soon discovered one of my guides seated a little above me, with a neat mat spread before him, which I supposed to be the place of honour and appropriated to strangers.

In a short time my people arrived and placed themselves

near me. The man by whom I sat immediately rose and from behind a plank of about four feet wide fetched a quantity of roasted salmon. He then directed a mat to be placed before me and Mr. Mackay who was sitting by me. When this ceremeony was performed, he brought a salmon for each of us and half a one to each of my men.

The signs of our protector seemed to denote that we might sleep in the house. From the fear of giving offence, I thought it prudent to order the men to make a fire without that we might sleep by it. When he observed our design, he placed boards for us that we might not take our repose on the bare ground, and ordered a fire to be prepared for us. We had not been long seated round it when we received a large dish of salmon roes, pounded fine and beat up with water, so as to have the appearance of a cream. Nor was it without some kind of seasoning that gave it a bitter taste. Another dish soon followed, the principal article of which was also salmon roes with a large proportion of gooseberries, and a herb that appeared to be sorrel. Its acidity rendered it more agreeable to my taste than the former preparation.

Having been regaled with these delicacies, for such they were considered by that hospitable spirit which provided them, we laid ourselves down to rest with no other canopy than the sky. I never enjoyed a more sound and refreshing rest though I had a board for my bed and a billet for my pillow.

After a 5 A.M. breakfast of gooseberries, hurtleberries, raspberries, roasted salmon and dried fish eggs, Mackenzie examined the fish weir. But, because he was a meat-eater and since they believed that the salmon would never return if they detected the slightest trace of flesh, the Indians would not allow him to come any closer than the river bank.

The dam, four feet above the water and filling the middle two-thirds of the fifty-yard milky stream, was made by fixing the trunks of small trees in the river bed when the water was low, covering these with gravel, adding more trees, another layer of gravel, and so on. On either side of the weir, timbered fish ladders and chutes led leaping salmon directly into traps. "At the foot of the fall dipping nets are also successfully employed."

So superstitious were these Indians about the behaviour of the salmon, that "one of my people having thrown a deer-bone into the river, a native immediately dived and brought it up, consigned it to the fire, and instantly proceeded to wash his polluted hands."

One of the mountain guides had obtained canoes for Mackenzie from these people, but departed homewards before the explorer could thank and reward him for his services. At one o'clock the expedition set out, joined by seven of the village Indians, who proved to be superb canoemen. "The stream was rapid, and ran upwards of six miles an hour. We came to a weir where the Indians landed us and then shot over it themselves without taking a drop of water. I had imagined that the Canadians who accompanied me were the most expert canoemen in the world, but they are very inferior to these people, as they themselves acknowledged, in conducting those vessels."

Two and a half hours later they were landed, and directed along a path to a large Indian village. Just before reaching the houses, Mackenzie was placed in the lead. His appearance created a minor alarm, but he strode into their midst with firm friendliness. He counted sixty-five men. "I shook hands as usual with such as were nearest me, when an elderly man broke through the crowd and took me in his arms. Another then came and paid me the same compliment." After considerable embracing, "a mark of regard and friendship," the eldest of the old chief's sons stepped forward, took off "a very handsome robe of sea-otter skin" which he was wearing, and put it round Mackenzie's shoulders.

Then they were feasted on roast salmon and some cakes, made from the inner rind of the hemlock tree and plentifully sprinkled with fresh salmon oil. Later, when he had his own shelter ready and could act the host, among the gifts presented by Mackenzie to the chief was a pair of scissors for trimming his long beard. The old man started snipping at once.

Next morning Mackenzie was shown the contents of the chief's treasure chest: a brass-buttoned garment of blue cloth, another of flowered cotton; various-shaped pieces of copper, brass, and iron; trinkets of all sorts; and daggers with a blade ten to twelve inches long and four inches wide tapering to a point, and with a silver coin fixed on the end of the handle.

Mackenzie toured the settlement. It was a big place. Besides a number of smaller kitchens or work sheds, there were eleven houses, four of them supported twelve feet above the ground on thick poles. These raised buildings were a hundred by forty feet with seven- or eight-foot walls, roofed with planks and bark. All round the inside they were divided into cedar-planked apartments seven feet square. The central open room, thus framed by sleeping quarters, held from three to five fires.

One structure in the middle of the village had sculptured frame props:

> The two centre posts at each end are two feet and a half in diameter and carved into human figures. They support two ridge poles on their heads twelve feet from the ground. The figures at the upper part of this square represent two persons with their hands upon their knees, as if they supported the weight with pain and difficulty. The others opposite to them stand at their ease, with their hands resting on their hips. The posts, poles and figures, were painted red and black.

The travellers passed the night here and by noon the next day Mackenzie was ready to leave. Everyone had now enjoyed plenty of food and rest, and they seemed to have won the goodwill of the Indians, which would secure their return. The young chief, eldest son of the village headman, was to go with them as a guide.

A canoe was provided. "This canoe was built of cedar, forty-five feet long, four feet wide, and three feet and a half in depth. It was painted black and decorated with white figures of fish of different kinds. The gunwale, fore and aft, was inlaid with the teeth of the sea-otter."

Before getting into the canoe, Mackenzie made a fuss about an axe which one of his men announced missing. He sat down on a stone and refused to budge until it was given back. It was found hidden under the chief's canoe. Although some of his followers thought it wrong to create a stir over such a small thing and perhaps offend the Indians, Mackenzie's view was that it would have been weakness to let them keep the axe, especially after pointedly noticing its loss. Ignoring its theft "might have occasioned the loss of everything we carried with us, and our lives also."

Finally the huge canoe was placed in the river, "almost one continued rapid," and they left the Great Village, as Mackenzie called it, of some two hundred persons. There were several other settlements along the Bella Coola. Some they stopped at, others they shot by. In the late afternoon "we came to a fall where we left our canoe, and carried our luggage along a road through a wood for some hundred yards. We came to a village consisting of six very large houses, erected on palisades, rising twenty-five feet from the ground."

It was Friday, July 19. "From these houses I could perceive the termination of the river, and its discharge into a narrow arm of the sea." He had come a long way to witness that sight, about fifteen hundred miles. And so, for a few moments, he stood and stared.

Chapter fourteen

The rock

N EXT MORNING the Great Village Indians refused to bring their canoe down the falls "as they imagined that I should be satisfied with having come in sight of the sea." Two of the four consented to go on with the expedition, one of them the young chief. "We obtained a larger canoe and though it was in a leaky state we were glad to possess it."

The stretch of salt water that Mackenzie saw first was North Bentinck Arm, ten miles long and about two wide. The landless horizon of the open Pacific was more than one hundred miles away through islands and channels. Mackenzie's curiosity to see a bit more got him into trouble.

About eight they were into "the narrow arm of the sea." The tide was out, baring a green seaweedy shore. The bulging hills were draped with fog. They headed into a strong west wind and a high swell. When they landed in a small cove near the mouth of North Bentinck Arm, the young chief and his companion announced that they were going to return. Mackenzie did not object; he asked only that the people along the river be told that he would be back in three nights.

But at dark the young chief reappeared, bearing a large porcupine on his back. He "first cut the animal open, and having disencumbered it of the entrails threw them into the sea. He then singed its skin and boiled it in separate pieces. With the assistance of two of my people who happened to be awake, every morsel of it was devoured."

For breakfast, although the Canadians had no desire to share them, "Mr. Mackay collected a quantity of small mussels which we boiled." Food supplies were perilously low—twenty pounds of pemmican, fifteen pounds of rice, and six pounds of flour—so the range of any coastal travel was obviously limited.

At six they paddled west out of North Bentinck Arm, turned north through Labouchere Channel for ten miles and then turned west again into Dean Channel, in order to find "a proper place for taking an observation." These bodies of water can be found only on a fairly large-scale map of the Ocean Falls–Bella Coola district.

As they coasted westerly along the southern shore of Dean Channel, they saw the approaching bows of "three canoes, with fifteen men in them." The boats were also loaded "with their moveables." Although these people spoke with a different accent, they "entered into conversation with our young man, as I supposed, to obtain some information concerning us." With swaggering contempt "they examined everything we had in our canoe."

One of these Indians, judging from Mackenzie's tale, had a grudge to settle with white men. From his manner, and tone, and signs, Mackenzie gathered "that a large canoe had lately been in this bay, with people in her like me, and that one of them whom he called *Macubah* had fired on him and his friends, and that *Bensins* had struck him on the back with the flat part of his sword. He illustrated these circumstances by the assistance of my gun and sword." *Macubah* is perhaps a mispronunciation of Vancouver. That captain had been nearby on June 2, but his published journal contains no record of any such happening.

After this show of resentment, all Mackenzie wanted to do was to get away from these men. He kept heading west, but without the young chief, who had been coaxed into one of the canoes. All three turned and tailed Mackenzie for six miles along Dean Channel. Here they met a canoe with two boys in it "who were dispatched to summon the people on that part of the coast to join them."

Now an Indian crew paddled right alongside. "The troublesome fellow forced himself into my canoe, pointed out a narrow channel on the opposite shore that led to his village, and requested us to steer towards it." Mackenzie gave the command and the canoe was turned towards Elcho Harbour, about half a mile wide and three miles deep, on the north side of Dean Channel.

The troublesome fellow "now became very irksome, and he wanted to see everything we had, particularly my instruments. He asked for my hat, my handkerchief, and in short everything that he saw about me. At the same time he frequently repeated the unpleasant intelligence that he had been shot at by people of my colour."

On the east shore of the harbour mouth Mackenzie noticed a large rock and beyond it a ruined village, deserted and overgrown with weeds. Just before or just after he saw the rock, he very likely also saw a squadron of Indian canoes knifing towards them out of Elcho Harbour. Suddenly, suspecting "some hostile design," Mackenzie made a snap decision. They would not risk entering the long narrow gullet of the harbour or visit the settlement at its end.

The steersman received a swift order. The Canadians were alerted. At just the right moment the canoe pulled sharply ahead to the safety of a miniature Gibraltar. They jumped out and "took possession of the rock where there was not space for more than twice our number and which admitted of our defending ourselves with advantage, in case we should be attacked."

He warned his men "to be very much upon their guard and to be prepared, if any violence was offered, to defend themselves to the last." They reached the confined surface with not a minute to spare. "We were soon followed by ten canoes, each of which contained three to six men."

Neither side was openly hostile, though the people in the three canoes who had dogged them all the way were bothersome and irritating. Eventually, with the young chief in their company, they left. "The rest of our visitors continued their pressing invitations to visit their village." Mackenzie refused, and much to everyone's relief they paddled away at sunset.

The natives having left us, we made a fire to warm ourselves. As for supper, there was but little of that for our whole daily allowance did not amount to what was sufficient for a single meal. The weather was clear throughout the day which was succeeded by a fine moon-lit night. I directed the people to keep watch by two in turn, and laid myself down on my cloak.

The hours of darkness passed unbroken by any sentinel's cry, and the day came on clear and pleasant. When a solitary Indian arrived with half a pound of seal's flesh to trade, finally accepting a few beads, Mackenzie concluded "that no general plan had been formed among the natives to annoy us." However he had already rung the warning alarm the day before, and his followers were still worried.

About eight in the morning a couple of canoes, "our young Indian along with them," brought some otter skins and raw seal's flesh which "hunger compelled my people to take at an extravagant price." Mackay lighted a bit of touch-wood in the cover of his tobacco-box with a burning-glass, which so surprised the natives that they exchanged the best of their otter skins for it.

The young chief urged flight, for "the natives, he said, were as numerous as mosquitoes and of a very malignant character." The men added their pleas, but Mackenzie stubbornly refused to listen. First he would find the latitude and longitude of the place. By rare fortune the weather on this wet, usually cloudy coast was clear.

At noon, while he stood measuring the sun's altitude, two large well-manned canoes came at them from the west along Dean Channel. The young chief frantically urged taking to the canoe "as they would soon shoot their arrows and hurl their spears at us. His agitation was so violent that he foamed at the mouth."

Unmoved by the panic around him, Mackenzie carefully completed his observations, although he allowed the men to load their craft. The Indians drew closer, landed, and disgorged five families. They were at once diverted by the white man's wonders—as Mackenzie perhaps expected—for "my instruments being exposed, they examined them with much apparent admiration and astonishment."

I now mixed up some vermillion in melted grease and inscribed in large characters on the South-East face of the rock on which we had slept last night, this brief memorial—"Alexander Mackenzie, from Canada, by land, the twenty-second of July, one thousand seven hundred and ninety-three." [Location of this rock was a fine piece of detective work. It is told in *Mackenzie's Rock* by R. P. Bishop, published in Ottawa in 1924.]

As I thought that we were too near the village, I consented to leave this place. We proceeded North-East three miles. We landed on a point in a small cove where we could not be readily seen and could not be attacked except in our front.

Around them solid rock rose three to seven hundred feet out of the sea. Down its sides trickled sweet ice-cold water.

The two canoes of Indians had followed them this far and when they collected themselves to go, the young chief got ready to join them. But Mackenzie "compelled him by force to come on shore. I thought it much better to incur his displeasure than to let him expose himself to any accident among strangers or to return to his father before us." Since the Canadians refused to accept the responsibility of guarding a chief's son, Mackenzie had to watch him.

After sunset Mackenzie obtained a longitude by focussing on Jupiter's satellites through his telescope. His observations were finished.

Now the expedition could begin to retrace its path to Peace River.

Chapter fifteen

Rascals and friends

T HE HOMEWARD journey began at ten in the evening. "Though the tide was running out very strong, we proceeded at a considerable rate by keeping close in with the rocks. My people were very anxious to get out of the reach of the inhabitants of the coast." So, they paddled furiously until well after sunrise. But, by a queer coincidence, not at the right speed to avoid "the inhabitants of the coast."

By four-thirty in the morning they turned into North Bentinck Arm and towards the village at the mouth of the Bella Coola River. When they reached the end of the inlet, "our guide directed us to draw the canoe out of the reach of the tide and to leave it."

He would not wait however till this operation was performed and I did not wish to let him go alone. I therefore followed him through a bad road encumbered with underwood. When we had quitted the wood and were in sight of the houses, I was surprised to see two men running towards me with daggers in their hands and fury in their aspect.

Mackenzie stopped short, threw down his cloak, and pointed his gun at them. He was lucky that the Indians knew what firearms could do. Their daggers, which were fastened by a string to their wrists, they let fall away. Shifting his gun to his left hand, Mackenzie drew his sword with his right. More Indians, also armed with daggers, reinforced those blocking the path to the village. "Among them I recognized the man whom I have already mentioned as being so troublesome to us, and who now repeated the name *Macubah* and *Benzins*, signifying at the same time by his action, as on a former occasion, that he had been shot at by them."

If Mackenzie didn't understand what he was saying, the others did; and it could well be that what he said actually restrained rather than excited their anger. The Indians sidled closer and one of them got behind Mackenzie and grabbed him. He fought free. Why he wasn't stabbed, he couldn't guess, and how long all this silent sparring took, his narrative does not record. Apparently the troublesome fellow's complaints were not so sore that they could only be soothed by murder.

One of my people now came out of the wood. On his appearance they instantly took to flight and with the utmost speed sought shelter in the houses. It was however upwards of ten minutes before all my people joined me. As they came one after the other, these people might have successively dispatched all of us and not one would have returned home to tell the horrid fate of his companions.

With his people gathered about him, Mackenzie was determined to have a showdown with the Indians—"to make these natives feel the impropriety of their conduct towards us." Most of the men from the three canoes first met in Dean Channel were in the village. Mackenzie was also determined to get back his hat and cloak, which had been taken during the scuffle on the path, and other articles which had been stolen while the expedition was on the rock by Elcho Harbour. "I therefore told my men to prime their pieces afresh and prepare themselves for an active use of them, should the occasion require it."

The expedition formed up in front of one of the houses. The young chief came out and was given a list of demands: the restoration of the stolen goods, food, and poles for pushing the canoe. The latter things, as well as the rental of the leaky canoe, would be paid for. The bluff carried. No shooting was necessary, and Mackenzie did not have to fight his way up the Bella Coola.

"A reconciliation now took place, but our guide or young chief was so terrified that he would remain no longer with us. He requested us to follow with his father's canoe." Shortly after noon they left the settlement, which Mackenzie named Rascals' Village.

With a small group, Mackenzie walked along the river bank. Four of the men poled the canoe up the rapids against a very strong current. He would have agreed to make the upriver journey by foot except that one of the hunters was so weak that it was impossible for him to walk.

In the meantime the native, who has been already mentioned as having treated us with so much insolence, and four of his companions went up the river in a canoe with as many boxes as men in her. This circumstance was the cause of fresh alarm, for it was generally concluded that they would produce the same mischief and danger in the villages above as they had in that below.

After an hour with the poles the Canadians met Mackenzie and his waiting group a mere half-mile up the river. The men refused to go any further. This time they were really afraid, desperately and uncontrollably afraid, and mutinously weary of fatigue itself. "The greater part of the men announced their determination to attempt the mountains, and try by passing over them to get to the road by which we came to the first village."

Mackenzie sat himself on a stone and waited for the fit of terror to wear itself out. Then he spoke. They had food for only two days. A mountain path would be cold and more tiring to travel than the river bank. Would they callously abandon the sick Indian hunter? Besides, their fears were unreasonable; the expedition was armed well enough to parry any threat. He persuaded them to give up the foolhardy scheme of leaving the populated Bella Coola road for an unknown or even nonexistent mountain trail.

They were won over. But most of them refused to continue the exhausting labour of poling the huge cedar canoe against the swift current. "My steersman, who had been with me five years, instantly replied that he was ready to follow me wherever I should go; but that he would never again enter that canoe, as he had solemnly sworn he would not while he was in the rapid."

However the vessel had to be returned to the chief of the Great Village. So Mackenzie, Mackay (who had stood steadfastly by his captain), the sick hunter, and two of the Canadians were left to cope with it themselves, grasping and pulling forward from one tree branch to another. The rest of the company walked along the river-bank trail, not moved by conscience or sympathy to offer any assistance.

The young chief, who had gone ahead, met them when they landed at a house. They were treated in a friendly way and given some fish. The next settlement was not reached until just before dark. "The turbulent Indian and his four companions" were the first persons they saw, but soon after the residents welcomed them with fish and berries.

That night they enjoyed their first sleep for at least forty strenuous, frightened hours. Mackenzie woke first and sent Mackay to check on the canoe. He returned to say that the Dean Channel Indians had loaded it with their goods and were preparing to depart. "I hurried to the waterside and seizing the canoe by the stern, I should certainly have overset it and turned the three men that were in it with all their merchandise into the river, had not one of the people of the house informed me that this was indeed their own canoe. My guide had gone off with ours." The "troublesome Indian" boarded and shoved off downstream. He was never seen again.

Soon after his arrival on the previous evening, Mackenzie had learned that "the Indians who had caused us so much alarm were inhabitants of the islands and traders in various articles such as cedar bark for weaving into mats, fish-spawn, copper, iron, and beads which they get on their coast. For these they receive in exchange roasted salmon, hemlock bark cakes, and the other made of salmon roes, sorrel, and bitter berries."

Three days before, Mackenzie had accidentally met these traders in Dean Channel with their canoes "laden with moveables." Then he had reacted with an annoyance that mounted to hostility and was climaxed by the expedition taking battle stations. Quite by chance they collided again on the river. And in this last fracas, Mackay and Mackenzie, tense, suspicious, tired and angry, assumed that the "bad" Indians were making off with their canoe and goods. They were wrong. How much of the fright and panic and rebellious discontent of his men was of Mackenzie's own making?

Now their canoe and guide were gone. They borrowed another and two Indians offered to help them pole upstream. Soon they met a fishing party and in it was a chief who had hosted them during a stop on their way to the sea. He took them to his houses, fed them, and arranged for their journey to two island houses where they camped the night. Most of the Canadians were still walking. The young chief had likely reached his home in the Great Village; it was the next settlement up the river.

In the morning they were taken further upstream and guided along a road beneath huge cedars twenty-four feet in circumference. Briefly they visited some deserted houses and paid a penalty for their nosiness. The cabin floors and the grass around the houses were crawling with fleas. Soon so were they. At the riverside they stripped and scrubbed themselves and their clothes thoroughly.

Under way again, they drew near to the Great Village. "As it was uncertain what our reception might be, I examined every man's arms and ammunition and gave Mr. Mackay, who had unfortunately lost his gun, one of my pistols." At one o'clock they arrived on the south bank opposite to the young chief's home. "Several of the natives were fishing above and below the weir, and they very readily took us over in their canoes."

As people gathered on the waterside, Mackenzie drew a line on the ground which he made it clear they must not cross. There were to be no embracing mobs this time. Mackenzie then went to look for the old chief. Should his life be in danger, he would fire two pistol shots. His men "were ordered to make the best of their way from these people."

Pistols loaded and stuck in his belt, dagger in hand, Mackenzie walked towards the chief's house. He didn't find him, but some women held out an offering of salmon roes and berries. Then "Mr. Mackay joined me, as my party were alarmed at my being alone."

Eventually the chief appeared with his son. The old man threw at Mackenzie a beaded tobacco pouch which had been stolen from Mackay. As he turned and walked away Mackenzie followed, shook the youth's hand without receiving any return warmth, ignored a peevish request for his sword, and joined the chief. "I took him and his son by their hands and asked them to come with me to my people."

I remunerated the young chief for his company and assistance in our voyage to the sea, as well as his father for his former attentions. I gave them cloth and knives and a portion of everything that now remained to us. The presents had the desired effect of restoring us to their favour. But these people are of so changeable a nature that there is no security with them.

When Mackenzie indicated that he was ready to depart, "the chief voluntarily sent for roasted salmon, and having attended us with his son and a great number of his people to the last house in the village, we took our leave. It was half past three in the afternoon."

They set out Indian file, Mackay in front and Mackenzie protecting the rear, still ready for trouble because of a rising noisy confusion in the village behind them. Some Indians, strangers who were visiting the village, dashed up and "made signs to me that we were taking a wrong road." The expedition remustered and finally got on the right path. It led them "through a forest of stately cedars."

At the village they had looked without success for their dog, who had been lost eight days before. Now he turned up, all skin and bones. The poor creature was very timid, approaching and then madly dashing away. They dropped some food for him and "by degrees he recovered his former sagacity."

When the night came on we stopped at a small distance from the river, but did not venture to make a fire. Every man took his tree and laid down in his clothes and with his gun. We had moved a short way from the path. No sentinel was appointed and every one was left to watch for his own safety.

At daybreak they started for the settlement "which we now called Friendly Village, and was the first we visited on our outward journey." They arrived at 8 A.M. The chief, Soocomlick, "entertained us with the most respectful hospitality. I presented him with two yards of blue cloth, an axe, knives, and various other articles. The chief, to his other acts of kindness, added as large a supply of fish as we chose to take." When they left at eleven, the villagers accompanied them for a mile.

Each man carried about twenty pounds of fish as they climbed the creek bed northerly out of the Bella Coola valley. It took them to the foot of a precipice. Here the creek, three feet deep, ran rapidly. "Our young Indian, though much recovered, was still too weak to cross the water. With some difficulty I carried him over on my back."

It was now one in the afternoon. As we had to ascend the first mountain before night came on in order to look for water and gather wood for a fire, I left the sick Indian with his companion and one of my men. It was past five when we arrived at a spot where we could get water. About seven our Indian and his companions arrived. We consoled ourselves by sitting round a blazing fire, talking of past dangers, and indulging the delightful reflection that we were thus far advanced on our homeward journey.

They were safe and relaxed at last, some four thousand feet above the Friendly Village, talking out their scares and frights and, in the camaraderie around the deep orange-embered heat and flickering whites and blues of the fire, cleansing their memories of the past week's mistakes, misgivings and discontents, and reviving their loyalties and their unity.

Those still evening hours of the journey were its triumphant, intoxicating climax.

Chapter sixteen

"We threw out a flag"

For THE PAST five years, when his mind had not been taken up with company affairs, the voyage to the shores of the Pacific had tyrannized Mackenzie's life and thoughts, and dictated his future. That hungry ambition was satisfied now. A simpler purpose drove the expedition—to travel swiftly and safely home to the Athabasca fort.

During the ten days needed to retrace the two-hundred-mile route to and along the West-Road River, the weather held fine. They recovered the buried pemmican. On Sunday afternoon, August 4, they arrived at their last Fraser River camp, not having met a single person the whole way.

The canoe was removed from its protective housing; and, except for some petty pilfering, the hidden stores of goods and provisions had not been touched. A rum keg was breeched and the celebrating dram served round the night fire, "but we had been so long without tasting any spirituous liquor that we had lost all relish for it." The loss was temporary.

Two days later, under cloudy skies, "we proceeded in high spirits on finding ourselves once more so comfortably together in the canoe." Other creatures were striving up the Fraser too, the salmon, "in such large shoals that the water seemed to be covered with the fins of them." Within a week they left the main branch of the Fraser River and ascended the McGregor River, like the salmon, struggling higher to the slow creeks and placid ponds on the very edge of the Great Divide.

The weather turned wet, raw, and cold. Wearily they carried around the rapids and tree-falls again or, walking in the river, pulled the canoe by line, until legs and feet were pain-numbed by the icy water.

112

The expedition recrossed the Divide on the sixteenth of the month and the next day, "at half past seven we began to glide along with the current" of the Parsnip River. The journey was nearly over now; and though they were always hungry, they had a home-flowing stream to their very doorstep. They had been twelve days getting up the Parsnip from its junction with the Peace; the river, swarming with beaver and wildfowl, swept them to the fork in two and a half days.

They re-entered the Peace River on the nineteenth and at noon the following day stopped and prepared to carry around the Peace River Canyon. They were near starving when they landed at the Rocky Mountain Portage, as it was called. The daily food allowance was barely enough for a single meal and there remained provisions for but two days. Mackay and the Indians were sent forward to hunt.

Five of the men began to carry the baggage, while the sixth and myself took the canoe asunder to cleanse her of the dirt, and expose her lining and timbers to the air, which would render her much lighter. About sunset Mr. Mackay and our hunters returned with heavy burdens of the flesh of a buffalo. Though not very tender, it was very acceptable.

By the morning of the twenty-second the portage, its difficulties increased by a fire which had obliterated in places the road they had carved out, had been surmounted. Large and small poles were prepared for coping with the rapids, and then the vessel was loaded. Mackay and the hunters went overland for game.

At seven Mackenzie and the Canadians embarked,

sometimes driving with the current, and at other times shooting the rapids. They had lost much of their former strength. Nevertheless we thought it necessary to land frequently to examine the rapids before we could venture to run them. However, the canoe being light, we fortunately passed them all and at noon arrived at the place where I appointed to meet Mr. Mackay and the hunters. There we found them with plenty of excellent fat meat, ready roasted, as they had killed two elks within a few hundred yards of the spot.

It was past one o'clock. Their hunger pangs temporarily relieved, everyone stepped into the canoe and they paddled off.

We saw animals grazing in every direction. In passing an island we fired at an elk and broke its leg. As it was now time to camp, we landed. The hunters pursued the wounded animal which had crossed to the mainland, but could not get up the bank. We went after it in the canoe and killed it.

To give some notion of our appetites, the elk carcass which we brought away weighed two hundred and fifty pounds. As we had taken a hearty meal at one o'clock, it might naturally be supposed that we should not be very hungry at supper. Nevertheless a kettle full of elk flesh was boiled and eaten, and that vessel replenished and put on the fire.

All that remained with bones &c. was placed after the Indian fashion round the fire to roast. And at ten next morning the whole was consumed by ten persons and a large dog who was allowed his share of the banquet. This is no exaggeration.

After another day's paddling, at their last camp of the voyage they tidied themselves up for their arrival at the fort near the Peace-Smoky junction.

1793

Saturday, August 24.—The weather was so warm that it was overwhelming and oppressive. The country increased in beauty; though as we approached the Fort, the animals appeared to diminish.

At length we rounded a point and came in view of the Fort. We threw out a flag and accompanied it with a general discharge of our fire-arms. The men were in such spirits and made such an active use of their paddles that we arrived before the two men, whom we left here in the spring, could recover their senses to answer us. Thus we landed at four in the afternoon at the place which we left on the ninth of May.

Here my voyages of discovery terminate. Their toils and their dangers, their solicitudes and sufferings, have not been exaggerated in my description. On the contrary, in many instances language has failed me in the attempt to describe them. I received, however, the reward of my labours, for they were crowned with success.

Chapter seventeen

Last years

DURING THE WINTER months of 1793-94 Mackenzie began to copy his journal. All the notes hastily pencilled in the canoe, at meal-stops, or by campfires had to be filled out, re-written, and shaped into story form. He wrote to his cousin Roderick that he found composition difficult. In that letter he sounds a bit like a schoolboy fretting over his homework.

> Last fall I was to begin copying my Journal. I took such a habit of thinking so long on a subject that I sometimes walked backward and forward, musing for hours.
>
> Did I sit down and write, the very things I ought not to have been thinking of would occur to me instead of what I had to do. This person calling me to the garret, another to the cellar, and others to the shop, kept me so busy doing nothing that my mind was never at ease. Nor could I bend it to my wishes.
>
> It was the end of January when I began my work. I will be satisfied, and so must you, if I can finish the copy for your perusal in the spring. I find it a work that requires more time than I was aware of, for it is not at this moment a quarter finished.

His notes were still "undigested" in the late fall. Between his return to Chepewyan from the West Coast and the printing of his journals eight years went by. Those years were not spent in the Northwest. "I think it unpardonable in any man to remain in this country who can afford to leave it." Mackenzie paddled out in the spring of 1794 and never returned. He had dreamed a great imperial and money-making dream. He hoped to make it come true.

Mackenzie believed he had found a suitable river road to the vast riches in fur and fish along the West Coast. A union of the Hudson's Bay and North West companies licensed to trade in the Far East; the closing down of the Montreal–Grand Portage–Lake Winnipeg route in favour of the cheaper Hudson Bay–Hayes River–Lake Winnipeg highway; the continued employment of French-Canadian personnel and birch bark canoes; the construction of trade posts and the establishment of a strong naval garrison on Pacific shores, would all make possible a powerful and profitable British monopoly of trade, resources, and territory—clear across the continent.

That vision was not realized in Mackenzie's lifetime. The two companies could not be brought together either by open or by secret dealing, or by the purchase of Hudson's Bay Company stock, and certainly not by any government's command. Mackenzie himself pursued an aggressively personal career. He joined with former wintering partners and for a few years entered into stiff competition with the North West Company. His X Y Company merged with its Montreal rival in 1804. Then for a short while he was even a member of the Legislative Assembly of Lower Canada. But that kind of politics did not appeal to him. Commerce was his whole life.

In 1808 he returned to Scotland, where in 1812 he married, purchased an estate, and more or less retired. After the publication of his travels he had become Sir Alexander Mackenzie. He died in 1820. The following year the bitter conflict between the Nor'westers and the Hudson's Bay Company was ended by the very union which Mackenzie had proposed more than a quarter of a century before.

His big achievements are plain. He opened up to trade and to further exploration three of Canada's great rivers. He first gave expression to the idea of a northern continental enterprise reaching from the Atlantic to the Pacific. And with his voyageurs from Quebec he first saw all of the three ocean waters beyond our shores.

What Champlain had looked for, Mackenzie had found.